The Ultimate Audition Book
for Teens Volume XI

111 One-Minute Monologues
by Type

Smith and Kraus
Monologue Books for Teens

MONOLOGUE BOOKS FOR MIDDLE SCHOOL ACTORS

Short Scenes and Monologues for Middle School Actors, Vol. I and II

The Ultimate Monologue Book for Middle School Actors:
>Vol. I: 111 One-Minute Monologues, by KRISTEN DABROWSKI
>Vol. II: 111 One-Minute Monologues, by JANET MILSTEIN
>Vol. III: 111 One-Minute Monologues, by L. E. MCCULLOUGH

AUDITION BOOKS FOR TEENS

The Ultimate Audition Book for Teens Series:
>Vol. I: 111 One-Minute Monologues, by JANET MILSTEIN
>Vol. II: 111 One-Minute Monologues, by L. E. MCCULLOUGH
>Vol. III: 111 One-Minute Monologues, by KRISTEN DABROWSKI
>Vol. IV: 111 One-Minute Monologues, by DEBBIE LAMEDMAN
>Vol. V: 111 Shakespeare Monologues for Teens, edited by LISA BANSAVAGE AND L. E. MCCULLOUGH
>Vol. VI: 111 One-Minute Monologues for Teens by Teens, edited by DEBBIE LAMEDMAN
>Vol. VII: 111 Monologues from Classical Theater, 2 Minutes & Under, edited by DEBBIE LAMEDMAN
>Vol. VIII: 111 Monologues from Classical Literature, 2 Minutes & Under, edited by DEBBIE LAMEDMAN
>Vol. IX: 111 Monologues from Contemporary Literature, 2 Minutes & Under, edited by DEBBIE LAMEDMAN
>Vol. X: 111 One-Minute Monologues for Teens by Teens, edited by KRISTEN DABROWSKI

OTHER ACTING BOOKS FOR TEENS

Great Monologues for Young Actors, Vol. I, II, and III

Hot Spots for Teens, Vol. I: One-Person Cold Reading Copy for TV Commercial Audition Success

Multicultural Monologues for Young Actors

Monologues in Dialect for Young Actors (dialects include Russian, American South, New York, Standard British, Cockney, and Irish)

The Spirit of America: Patriotic Monologues and Speeches for Middle and High School Students

Teens Speak Series, by KRISTEN DABROWSKI:
>Girls Ages 13–15: Sixty Original Character Monologues
>Boys Ages 13–15: Sixty Original Character Monologues
>Girls Ages 16–18: Sixty Original Character Monologues
>Boys Ages 16–18: Sixty Original Character Monologues

If you require prepublication information about upcoming Smith and Kraus books, you may receive our annual catalogue, free of charge, by sending your name and address to *Smith and Kraus Catalogue, PO Box 127, Lyme, NH 03768. Call us at (888) 282-2881; fax (603) 643-1831; or visit us at SmithandKraus.com.*

The Ultimate Audition Book for Teens VOLUME XI

• • •

111 One-Minute Monologues by Type

Kristen Dabrowski

YOUNG ACTORS SERIES

A Smith and Kraus Book

To Deborah and Amy for all their encouragement

A Smith and Kraus Book
Published by Smith and Kraus, Inc.
177 Lyme Road, Hanover, NH 03755
www.smithandkraus.com

First Edition: March 2007
Manufactured in the United States of America
10 9 8 7 6 5 4 3 2 1

Cover and text design by Julia Gignoux, Freedom Hill Design

ISBN 1-57525-529-4
ISBN 978-1-57525-529-3

Library of Congress Control Number: 2007920843

CONTENTS

Introduction .vii

MONOLOGUES BY CHARACTER TYPE

Activist 1
Addict 5
Airhead 10
Beauty Queen 11
Chatterbox .12
Class Clown 17
Control Freak 21
Drama Queen 24
Dreamer 27
Emo 29
Fan 30
Follower 33
Geek 35
Good Girl 39
Good Guy 42
Jealous Sibling 46
Jock 48
Material Girl 51
Misfit 52
Party Girl 58
Perfectionist 59
Player 63
Popular 65

Poser 70
Pothead 72
Protector 73
Rebel 75
Romantic .80
Slacker 85
Slob 89
Spaz 90
Teen Mother 91
Tomboy 92
Troublemaker 93
Victim 98
Visionary .102
Voice of Reason 103
Wannabe .107
Worrier 111

Subject Index 112

Introduction

Hello, actors! *This book is about making the search for the perfect monologue easier.* To make this possible, it's been organized in two ways:

The monologues arc divided up by *character type* presented in alphabetical order. However, categories are simple and people are complex. Keep this in mind when acting out these pieces. Bring as much humanity and variation to the characters as you can. Just like you, they contain layers. Remember, the purpose of this organization is not to fit people into convenient labels or stereotypes. (As John Hughes so rightly said in *The Breakfast Club,* "Each one of us is a brain, and an athlete, and a basket case, a princess, and a criminal.") It's merely to make the search for a monologue easier.

Additionally, there is also a *subject index* in the back. Feel free to flip through and see if there's a particular issue that "speaks" to you. Several monologues are purposefully difficult subject matters presented for actors seeking a challenge. Though it is never a bad choice to choose a monologue close to your issues and personality, each human being in the world has the capacity to imagine and to empathize with others. Don't be afraid to stretch yourself!

Here are some tips on approaching monologues:

- Pick the monologue that hits you. Trust your instincts. You'll pick the right one!

- Make the monologue active. Think about what you want (sympathy, a date, etc.), and how you try to get it (flattery, guilt, etc.).

- Who are you talking to and where are they? Some monologues have you speaking to more than one person. Make sure you make this as clear as possible.

- Do you get answered or interrupted? Be sure to fill in words in your head for the moments when you are spoken to in the monologue, even if it's a simple "yes" or "no."

- How do you feel about the person or people you are talking to? For example, you speak a lot differently to your best friend than you do to your math teacher.

- Be real. Talk like a real person. Think about how you'd feel in the same circumstances. Bring these characters to life as only you can.

These monologues stand alone as solo pieces (and are not from full-length plays). However, if you want to put together a showcase of monologues, you'll see that some pieces work very well together. Feel free to mix and match.

Additionally, if you'd like to change a word or the gender of a character, etc., feel free. I want these monologues to work for you!

Enjoy!

Kristen Dabrowski

THE DEBATE

LYRA is interested in politics, and so is her father. However, they are on different sides of the political fence. Her father greatly disagrees with her beliefs to the extent that he is unable to listen to her viewpoints.

I want to go to the rally! This is important to me. This war— Where are you going? This conversation *isn't* over! It's just begun. It's not going to be dangerous, Dad. It's a *peace* rally. Think about it. If you want to come with me, you can. If you're so worried about my safety. Maybe you'll even learn something new! Please, Dad, I really want to go!

Mom, why is he like that? Why am I not allowed to have a different opinion from him? Why should I always agree? Do you want me to think for myself or to be a robot? I'm not him. I can't be him. I don't want to be him! We're different. I don't see why that makes him so angry. Am I really so awful and threatening to him? Am I such a disappointment?

That *is* what he thinks! Why else would he get so mad when I don't do everything he says? He's just disappointed that I'm not what he wants me to be. Do you know what it's like living with the idea that you are always a disappointment? It's not fun, Mom.

OPEN

GREG is a fiery and passionate Republican living in a liberal household.

Did you ever just hate your parents? Well, I do. Just now. I hate them. You just cannot talk to people like that. They are so unreasonable. I am so mad! I was just in the kitchen with them, trying to have an adult conversation about politics, and my dad happens not to agree with me. Can we debate? No. He's got to get in my grill and start yelling—right away!—about how I'm wrong and how the president blah blah blah. He's totally a mouthpiece for the liberal media. He's so brainwashed that he can't even open his mind to other possibilities. And he's clearly not listening to me. And my mom! She just sits there, all meek and dumb. Whatever! They are such suckers! Completely believe whatever the stupid news says. How can a person even know what the truth is anymore? It seems like everyone lies. They're so stupid it drives me crazy. How can I be under the same roof as people who are closed-minded! God!

PRINCIPLES

BROOKE is a socially conscious liberal who refuses to do a school assignment that conflicts with her political beliefs.

I'm not doing this. I don't care if I fail the class. This is disgusting and wrong. I'm not writing this essay. I don't want to support our troops. I think war is wrong, no matter what. It's wrong to kill other people. That's why we send murderers to jail. So why are these soldiers any different? They're *not*. They're killers. So I am not going to write some rah-rah speech for some stupid contest about how I think our troops, who are essentially contract *killer*s, are so fantastic. How brave is it to stand with a machine gun and gun someone down? Do they look each other in the eyes? We have to see people as *individuals*. A person is not where they are from. A person is not what side of a border they live on. Borders were just randomly drawn on a map by some guy at a desk. Why should I be so proud of which side I'm on? Why should anyone risk and possibly end their lives for them? Think about it! It just doesn't make sense. People have *souls*. I could never, ever take a human life, especially for some dumb political reason, and I cannot and will not support anyone who does!

Fine! I'll go to the principal! It's better than being in here. You people are intolerant and ignorant!

MR. PINK PANTS

INGRID is a freshman in college and an advocate for women's rights. When a guy asks her advice for doing laundry, she is shocked and offended.

How should I know? Because I'm a girl I'm supposed to know how to do laundry? Is this the Dark Ages? I don't know any more about laundry than you do.

Maybe I don't wash my own "little dresses." That makes me spoiled? Why don't you know how to do your laundry? Your mom does it. Why is it if my mom does my laundry I'm spoiled, and if your mom does—You're a mama's boy. You are! And you're a male chauvinist pig.

Wait! I think I know a little bit about laundry. I remember a thing or two. Wash everything on hot, so they get really clean. And you need to use a *lot* of laundry detergent. Put all the clothes you can in one washer to save money. Put reds with whites, not darks. That way they don't turn purple. OK?

(The guy walks away.) Can you believe that jerk?

PLUGGED IN

ROB is so attached to his computer that he no longer feels he needs to interact with the actual, physical world outside his door. Plus, his preferred web content is getting more and more extreme. His addiction is porn.

I just don't see the point of going outside anymore. I have all I need in here. Basically, my whole life is in my computer. All my friends are here, all my activities . . . There's really no point in school or anything like that anymore. That's the past. This is the future. You can stay at home and learn all you want on the net. And you can be whoever you want. Like, see, here's KandiKane88. She thinks I'm six-three and a quarterback on a college team. I've been a pilot, a model, an actor, a musician—Basically, I can be whatever and whoever I want. No one questions me. It's brilliant. And I can get anything I want. Girls take off their clothes for me. I admit, I have a little . . . problem with that. If you think that kind of thing is a problem. Thankfully, my mom is completely ignorant about the computer. But I really like the porn sites. I see it as research. The human body is a natural thing, right? I'm a young guy. I'm supposed to be interested in this stuff. I can't help that it's so accessible. And if these girls didn't want to do this, they wouldn't. So I don't feel bad about it. I don't see why it's such a bad thing. In fact, I think it's a really, really, *really* excellent thing. Thank God for the Internet.

CRASH

ISAAC is a high-energy, fast-talking coffee addict who has not had his fix for several hours now.

I have such a headache. I need a coffee right now. My head is just pounding! I think it's a crime that the school doesn't serve coffee. I need to be supplied! I am not addicted. I just like it. It has no effect on me. None at all. I don't feel energized or nervous or anything. I just feel normal. I've always talked fast! That's not the coffee! I just have a lot of energy. Except not now. I feel like I'm going to fall asleep. Yes, this is how I talk when I'm tired! Shut up! I'm never going to make it through bio if I don't get some java now. Do you think there's enough time to sneak out and get some? This is an emergency. Please drive me into town? Come on. We won't get caught. This is an *emergency*.

I'm not addicted! I can stop anytime I want!

CARPEL TUNNEL WARRIOR

BERNIE plays video games night and day. He has an aggressive, enthusiastic personality and imagines he's the ultimate soldier.

Man, I wish I was old enough to be sent to war. I'd be awesome. I'd be a great sniper. You've seen me blast my way through video games. I've got great control. I can *sense* when someone's coming. I was *made* for combat, I think. I've got everything it takes. I'm cool, steady, and ready to go.

Man, I'd love to blast my way through Baghdad. Blow a hole in everything that comes my way. Make my family and my country proud.

Sure, I'd die! Imagine what a hero I'd be if I did. I'd be dying for all the right things. Regular people die of heart attacks and shit, but I'd be dying for a *reason*. It would be worth it. If there weren't soldiers to protect this country, we'd be Communists or speaking Chinese or some such shit. But I honestly don't think anything would happen to me. I have the skills, and I am ready for action!

Want to go another game? What's the matter? Chicken?

THINK LESS OF ME

ALISHA is a constant dieter. As a result, she thinks about food 24/7 and worries constantly about what to eat and what people think of her food choices.

Oh my god, I want a doughnut so bad! I hate being on a diet. I don't understand why I can't be one of those girls who's born skinny. It's not fair. Why do I have to be that girl on a diet all the time? I swear, I could eat a dozen of those. Why do they sell them at school? The temptation is too much. I have absolutely no willpower. When something is plopped in front of me, I have to eat it. It's not fair.

I do not eat too much crap! You don't know how often I don't eat things. But I want to be a regular teenager, too. I want to eat pizza and drink sodas and be a regular kid, too. I don't want to be separate from everyone else. It makes people look at me when I say no to those things. "Why don't you want a piece of cake, Carla?" "Don't you even want a little?" People look at me like I'm some kind of freak. But at the same time, if I start eating like other, normal girls, people look at me like, "What a fat pig." I just can't win! I hate being in this body! I wish I could get plastic surgery. My life is so unfair.

LOOK AWAY, COME CLOSER

JENNY is confused, angry, scared, and a cutter. Her parents have made her come to an appointment with a psychiatrist.

Listen, I don't want to talk to you. I don't see why I have to. I don't even know you. My mom made me come here. Even my dad thinks this is a load of crap. So, you're just going to sit there and stare at me?

Well, yeah, I'm angry. I have to come here! I don't want to come here. I'm not mental or anything. I'm fine. I mean, my life sucks, but what's new? Who doesn't have problems?

I don't want to talk about that. I don't know why I do it anyway. I just do. It's something I like to do, OK? I *enjoy* it. If you and my mom don't get that, that's your problem. Why should I have to explain it to you? I'm not hurting anyone.

It doesn't hurt. I cut myself to stop it hurting. Physical hurt is nothing. I can take that. The cuts are nothing. It's what's inside—See, you got me talking. You must think you're clever. But I'm done now.

SOMETHING'S MISSING

RACHEL is very likable and good-natured, but hopelessly ditzy a lot of the time. This is a typical morning for her.

Where are my shoes? Hey, has anyone seen my shoes? You know which ones; the ones I wear all the time! I don't know where I left them. If I did, I would just find them. I lose everything, I know! I can't help it. I'm just made that way. Spacey. I'd lose my nails if they weren't glued on. Lizzie, did you borrow my blue sweater? Oh my god, I'm wearing it! Never mind! Do you think I'm too old to have those little clips that attach mittens to my coat? Which reminds me, Mom, I lost my gloves again! I know it's the fourth time this winter. But gloves are like socks and sunglasses. I swear, they walk off on their own.

Ooo, that reminds me. Lizzie, your ex called last night. Sorry! I forgot! I was on the phone with Lindsey because this girl in gym class said to her—

OK! OK! I'm moving, Mom. What's the hurry? It's what time? Whoops! OK! I'm ready! Let's go! Oh, yeah, my shoes! Can you guys please help me find my shoes?

AND THE WINNER IS . . .

MARLEEN is deeply invested in the pageant world. Other people in her school don't get it and give her a hard time about it.

What's wrong with being a pageant queen? It is not *fake*; it's real. And it's not a beauty contest. The interview is a huge part of your score and whether you win. If you don't get good grades in school, and you don't do well in the interview, you won't win. Don't you watch Miss America? Those girls win scholarships for a reason. Well, yes, an ordinary-looking girl could win. Sure. It could happen!

It's not creepy! This is *normal*. It makes me feel good about myself. It makes me feel important. When you win, it's the best thing in the world. You get prizes and a crown, and you know people like you. That's good for your self-esteem.

Well, now you're just being rude. Maybe we should talk about something else now because I am about to lose my . . . composure. Excuse me, please.

CAMP

MATT is a counselor at a summer camp who's never spent time away from his family before. He tends to jump from subject to subject quickly without necessarily waiting for a response.

Have you ever been away from home before? I haven't. It's strange. I'm annoyed all the time at home by my parents, my sister, my brother . . . But when I get here . . . I miss them a little. I don't know. I guess just because nothing's familiar.

Man, I'd love to sleep in my bed for one night. My back is killing me. And a little privacy would be nice! I haven't slept in a bunk bed since I was six. I almost fell on my face this morning getting out of bed.

When I signed up to be a counselor, I wasn't betting on all of this. *Walking* thirty feet to the bathroom in the middle of the night? I'm so glad my parents didn't make me go to camp when I was a kid.

When do we get to meet some girls?

ABOMINABLE

DANA is a talkative girl with a quiet best friend who acts as the soundboard for Dana's ideas. Her subject today is body hair.

I wish I could get the hair lasered off my legs. Think of how much time that would save in the shower! Not to mention that you'd never have to freak out in the winter on those days when you forget you have gym class. Sure, it's high maintenance at first, but you'd save so much time in the long run. It's too bad it's so expensive. Do you think there's any way I could convince my mom that I need it? Some girls hardly have any hair at all. I'm like a yeti. You could braid the hair on my arms! I really need this. I don't want to shave and wax for the rest of my life. Just the thought of waxing—ouch!

Why is it so hard and so expensive and so time-consuming just to look normal? For me, at least. Some people just seem like they were born normal. For me, I have to do so much just to get by. Beautiful people can wear sloppy clothes and no makeup and look fine. Me, I have to get up early every day and do my hair and my makeup—It is so hard to find clothes that fit, too! OK, OK. Let's get back to the point. How can I get my mom to pay for laser hair removal? Come on, Lisa; don't just sit there! Participate in the conversation, please.

SO HOT

LES loves the sound of his own voice and never, ever stops talking. He will talk to anyone, anytime about anything.

Oh my god, I'm so hot, but not in a good way, know what I mean? What's up with that? Is this, like, global warming? Do you think that's real? And if it's real, then how can the warming of the globe bring about another ice age? I don't get it. Can you imagine being a dinosaur during an ice age, and you're just standing there and it's, like, "Oh my god, here comes the ice? Where do I go? What do I do?" Do you think it was that fast?

You know, all this talk about ice is cooling me down. Isn't that awesome? I'm like a genius! Mind over matter! The power of my mind is awesome, I swear.

Is something wrong? You're, like, holding your head and rolling your eyes. Should I call 911 or something? Maybe you're dehydrated or something. Drink some water! Somebody get this guy some water, he's like having an attack or something!

GIRLS' NIGHT OUT

ANITA is outgoing, flirty, and a little bit vain. When she sees a guy looking at her at a party, she confidently approaches him.

Hey, I saw you looking at me. How are you? I'm Anita. Great party, huh? You are really cute. I mean it. Do you have a girlfriend? No? Excellent! So, do you want to go out sometime?

No? That's it. No. You're not going to say why or anything? Are you gay? Just no. You're a pig, do you know that? It took a lot of guts for me to walk over here and talk to you. And I only did it because you were flirting with me. Why would you flirt with me for no reason? Do you get off on making girls feel stupid? You are such a jerk. You know, you're not really that good looking. I just said that. I didn't even think you were cute. My friend did, so I decided to take a chance that maybe you were a nice guy. Boy, was I wrong!

Which friend? My friend with the brown curly hair. Why? You were flirting with *her*? Are you serious? Well, I'm going to tell her you're a pig. Too bad you weren't nicer to me, assface. Maybe I would have set you up with her. I hope you learned something today.

THAT GIRL

ARIELLE is waiting for a phone call from a guy she really likes. She prides herself on being a strong, independent person, but can't resist being "that girl" who sits around waiting for a phone call.

This is pathetic. I can't believe I'm *that* girl. I'm *that* girl! Sitting around waiting for the phone call. Pathetic. I'm such a cliché. I hate myself! Why am I like this? I don't know why I'm like this. I don't even like him *that* much. OK, I do. And that's the problem! Why do I like him so much? Why am I so desperate? I mean, I am and I'm not. I know I won't *die* if he doesn't call. But I really, *really* want him to! And I don't understand why he wouldn't call. It's been *four* days since our date. And it was good! We laughed, conversation was easy, I mean, it was all good! Why isn't the phone ringing?

Oh, the net! I haven't checked the net in . . . well, the last five minutes. But maybe he *wrote* me! That's easier, right? No awkward conversation. He e-mailed me I bet. Hurry up, computer! Check mail! Nothing. Check again! Oh my god, he didn't email me either. I have got to get a grip. He's not that funny. And I hate the way he runs. His feet look all wrong. I don't need him. Look, let's get out of here. Let's go somewhere. I'm fine. I'm not waiting anymore. Who needs Paul? He's a loser.

(Phone rings.) Oh my god! The phone! I love Paul! I love him!

THE HOUSE ON THE HILL

ERIN's friend wants to explore a rumored haunted house. Erin can't resist making a joke out of it.

I don't know about this. What if it's true? This place creeps me out. It's abandoned for a reason.

No, I don't believe it's haunted! Don't be stupid. It's just that it doesn't seem safe. I'm not superstitious, you know. I don't believe that crap.

Stop making those noises! You're an idiot. Be quiet! If we get caught, we could probably get arrested for trespassing or something. If we're going to do this, let's hurry up about it. Let's go upstairs, prove there are no ghosts, and go home. It's getting cold.

Do you hear that? Oh my god. A voice. Shhh! Do you hear that? It's the sound of . . . nothing at all! OK? Satisfied? Let's go, dimwit.

COME FLY WITH ME

CLARK KENT is used to jokes about being Superman. He's decided to go with it and try to use his parents' perverse name choice to try to pick up girls.

Um, yeah. I'm Clark Kent. You know, Superman? Secret's out! I swear! So, want to go out Saturday? I promise not to use my x-ray vision on you. Not that I wouldn't want to—I mean that in a good way! There's a slight possibility I might have to go solve some crimes in the middle of dinner, but, you know, I'd be right back if that happened.

Yeah, it is pretty dangerous. The bad guys never rest. But I manage.

The tights? Well, I tried it without them, but it looked wrong. Hairy legs really distract from the image. Somehow the look doesn't have the same *power* without the tights. And jeans—well, they're just too restrictive. We superheroes actually wear tights for a reason. They're practical.

So, should I pick you up at six?

THE DRESS

DONNA made the decision to wear a polyester mini-dress that she bought at a thrift shop without really thinking it through.

Why didn't anyone tell me that wearing polyester is like sticking your entire body in a furnace? Man, I thought this retro dress was cool, but I am sweating like a pig in July. Do I smell? Smell my pits. Is it bad? Come on, be a friend. Come on, Kara! I'd do it for you. OK, I wouldn't. But you're a better person than me.

Aw, I'm getting hives. I itch all over. Man, I need some calamine lotion. Where's my mom when I need her?

Hey! There's Colin Riley. I love him. Do you think Colin Riley would rub calamine lotion on me? I swear, I dream about him. He looks really good tonight. *Really* good.

Now I'm hotter than ever! Damn you, Colin Riley! I gotta get rid of this dress! I'll trade my clothes for yours. Come on! It's really not that bad. I was kidding. I'd do it for you, Kara!

TEAM PLAYER

CALEB is that guy who always accepts a dare. He wants to amuse and please his friends and often does crazy things for attention.

I'm twenty-one! I've been twenty-one for months now. I just forgot my ID at home. I walked here. Trust me. Why would I lie? It's just a six-pack. It's not like I'm going to go get drunk on this. It's actually for my dad. He loves beer. I don't actually like it very much. Weird, huh? But it's true. I don't like alcohol at all. He's going to be very upset with me if I don't get this. Look, I'm really sorry I forgot my ID. Next time I'll be sure to bring it with me. I promise.

I didn't want to tell you this, but my dad gets really mad when I don't do what he says. Know what I mean? Do you really want to send me home without this six-pack? Do you? God, what a jerk!

Sorry, guys, he wouldn't go for it.

POSSESSION

SEAN is possessive, jealous, and controlling. He is very afraid of being betrayed or made to look foolish.

That guy was rubbing up against you. What was that? That is not what I want to see my girlfriend doing with some random guy. Who is he? Do you know him? What the hell do you think you're doing? I'm standing *right here.* You need some manners. Step back and think before you go doing dirty things like that with some other guy.

Yeah, I said dirty! You weren't, like, ballroom dancing! You were grinding up against him. That is not a thing I want to see. Do you understand that? Do you know what something like that does to me? It makes me mad. It makes me real mad. I don't know. I don't know about you.

If you want me to stick around, maybe we ought to make some rules. Like *do not do that*! It's simple. You have to respect me. Hey, if you don't know how to do that, I'll tell you how. I've got no problem with that. But you'd better listen because I am not going to take that kind of behavior. That has got to stop.

IT'S MY PARTY, BIATCH

LUCY needs to be the center of attention on most occasions, and today is her birthday. When she spots a friend flirting with a guy she likes, she is not happy.

This is my party. *Mine.* You don't get to flirt with the guys I like. It's my *birthday*. Get it? This is *my time*. Not yours! How can you be so selfish? I'm not going to let you or anyone ruin my day. So you can just get out now.

I'm serious! Go! I don't want you here. You're ruining my day. I want to feel good today. I'm supposed to be the center of attention. And you are ruining everything, so you need to go.

We *were* friends, Jenna. We're not friends now. I can't be friends with someone who'd try to screw up my birthday party.

I *am* serious! You need to go! OK, fine! If you will stop being a jerk, I will let you stay. But if I so much as see you *looking* at a guy I like, you are out of here. I am serious, Jenna. This is *my* day, and I'll be damned if I let you spoil it.

HANDS OFF

JARED recently bought a car with the earnings from his after-school job. This is the first thing he's ever bought with his own money, and he does not want anyone or anything to touch it, including his father and his tools.

Dad, don't touch my car. I hate to put it like that, but this is *my* car. I worked for it; I paid for it. I know you mean well, I do, but I want to be responsible for this. I want it to be all mine. Can you understand that? Well, I appreciate the effort and the advice and all, but, uh, how can I put this? You are not a mechanic, Dad. Don't get mad! I don't mean it like that. It didn't come out right. I just mean you are not the best person at fixing cars. OK, that didn't sound right, either. I know I'm not an expert! I didn't say I was! All I know is every time you "fix" my car, it always runs worse afterward. It's true! I'm sorry to have to tell you the truth. Maybe I *am* ungrateful. But the point is, this is *my* car. And if I'm going to make mistakes and run it into the ground, I want it to be *my* mistake. Just don't touch my car, OK? I don't touch yours. I'm sorry to say it like that, Dad, but you just don't listen to me.

I'm not kidding! Put the tools down, Dad.

JUST YOU WAIT

> GABY *is a passionate, determined singer/actress who feels she's been slighted and overlooked by her egotistical drama teacher.*

I hate that witch. She doesn't know what talent is. I'm talented. I know I am. Aren't I? I know I can sing. Everyone tells me when I perform how good I am. So how can I only have a *minor* role? Just because I don't kiss her fat butt? She's jealous, I think. I mean, she's just teaching at a school. She never got famous. She never went to Broadway. What does she know?

It's all politics. I just can't be that kind of person who pretends to like someone when I don't. I know I should. I'd probably be the star of the show if I did that kind of thing. But it literally makes my skin crawl. She's vomitous.

One of these days, I'm going to get a huge award, and I'm going to tell the whole what a stupid, fat ass she was to me back in high school. She'll be sorry someday.

THE END

JORDAN just found out she did not get the lead in the play that she was counting on. As a result, she's lost her nerve and her confidence.

I really thought this was my year. This was the perfect play and the perfect part. So why didn't I get it? I'm graduating never having had a leading role now. How pathetic is that? Maybe I just don't understand what good is. Maybe I'm totally off in everything I think. Maybe I'm really horrifically awful, and I don't even know it, like those people who audition for *American Idol*. I'm so embarrassed! I've always thought—This is my dream, Desiree. This is the dream I've had since I was little. Why do I have this dream if I can't make it come true? I don't understand. I was *so* right for this!

Tell me the truth. Am I bad? No, it's useless. I'm sorry, but I don't even believe you. I can't believe you. Oh, I don't know! I don't know what to believe anymore! Maybe everyone's been lying to me all these years. Maybe everything I think is wrong.

It's not fair! My life is ruined now!

BEAST

DESTINY is having a mild allergic reaction but has a major response to the effect it's having on her skin.

I think I'm having an allergic reaction, Sandy! This is a disaster. I can't leave this room *ever*. Look at me! I'm all blotchy and itchy. There are white bumps and red dots all over me! Look at my eyes. They're all puffy. No one can see me like this. What could have done this? I've never been allergic to anything. Do you think it could be my new eye shadow? Oh god, I'm disfigured! I am! It *is* that bad. I can feel it. It's getting worse.

You *can* see it. It's really nice that you're telling me it's invisible, but I have eyes, Sandy, and I can see how hideous I look. A real friend wouldn't lie to me. I *know* you're trying to make me feel better, but you can't. I look like the Elephant Man. This is pure social disaster. Why did this disease have to attack my face? I am *not* being melodramatic, Sandy. I am being *real*. I am trying to face reality. I am trying to deal with the fact that I look like a freak now. Maybe you should just leave me alone. Maybe I need to get used to being alone now that I'm such a hideous freak! Just go, Sandy! Go! Leave me alone!

LOVE WITH THE PERFECT SUPERMODEL

KENNETH is unrealistic and immature for his age. He's not ready for a real romantic relationship, so he dreams of celebrities and models instead.

Are you in love or something? That's so weird. No way! I've never been in love. I can't even imagine. Shut up! I am not a loser! I am waiting for my Playboy model to come along. Oh, she will. Believe me. High school girls don't do it for me. I want like an Ashton/Demi-type thing. An older woman. I think that's sexy! You don't? You mean, if a hot, older woman like Angelina Jolie came along, and she was into you, you'd be like, "No thanks, I've got this high school girl-friend. I'm not interested." That's what you'd say? Now that's crazy, and you know it. No way would anyone say no to Angelina Jolie—those lips, that smokin' body? You *must* be in love. That's just crazy. If Angelina Jolie comes up to me, I would be like, "Hell, yeah, baby, let's go!" It could happen! It could! Shut up. Like you know about women. Give me a break.

PARADISE

SUZANNA lives in Minnesota and dreams of year-round tropical weather. She works to get her mother to see her point of view.

Can we move to Hawaii? Why not? I *am* being serious. I don't see why not. Just get a job there. How hard could it be? Think about it, Mom. Theoretically, you could live any-where. All you need is a job. So if you could live anywhere, where would you go? Hawaii, right? I've had enough of these snowy winters. I don't want to do this anymore. Can you imagine never having to wear a coat? Or shovel a side-walk? Sounds good, doesn't it? We could sit on the beach having drinks with umbrellas in them. Mine would be alco-holic, of course. And I would wear a bikini with a coconut top. Man, that's the life. We don't have that much stuff; it would be easy to pick up and go. If I looked for jobs for you on the Internet, would you consider it? It *can* happen, Mom. You have to think positive. Just keep thinking about those sandy beaches, Mom, every time you step out into the snow. We could live in paradise if we just worked on it a little.

FREEDOM OF DEPRESSION

*ROSS is an edgy musician who wears black and broods.
His mother worries that his "look" sends people the wrong
message and wishes he'd just dress like everyone else.*

It doesn't mean there's something wrong with me. I'm not
gay or on drugs or suicidal. I'm a *musician*. This is just a
style. Other people do it. People aren't going to "think
things." If people are that small minded, they can think
whatever they want. Why should I care what they think? You
worry too much about what people think of you. Who cares?
Be an individual. Stand out. I feel like I live in Gaptown,
where everyone wears the same things and does the same
things—it's *boring*. That's the problem with this whole country! Sure, a melting pot *sounds* like good, and I *like* the idea
that everyone gets along, but what really end up happening is
everyone tries to be the same. I don't want to be the same as
everyone else, Mom. And part of that is wearing black or
blue nail polish if I want. It's very rock and roll, and I like it.
It doesn't *mean* anything. It's just something I like to do. No,
I won't take it off! Ever heard of freedom of expression,
Mom? This is America, remember?

IN THE DRIVER'S SEAT

JON is a sports fanatic. In particular, he loves NASCAR. His girlfriend doesn't get it.

What do you mean, why do I like this? I don't know. It's just fun. It's interesting. It's not just people driving in circles. There's skill involved. And you get to know the drivers, so there's the whole thing where you want one person to win. And that's why it's interesting. That's why I like it.

Yeah, that's it. Well, there is one more thing. It's the possibility of a crash. I mean, everything's more exciting when you think someone might die. Life and death—that's about as good as it gets. So how can *you* not like this? That's the real question. How can shopping even come close to this?

I told you, I'm watching 'til the end of this race. If you want to go to the mall so bad, just go. This might shock you, but I really don't care about anything in the mall. So maybe you should tell *me* why you like *that*.

But not now. Commercial's over. I'm watching.

CALLER #25

EMILY just won tickets and backstage passes to her favorite singer's concert.

I won? I won? Are you serious? Are you kidding me? I won? Oh my god! I won! Oh my—So I get to meet him? In person? After the concert? So he'll be all sweaty. Oh my god. I don't know if I can handle this! No! No! Don't give it away to someone else. I can do this. Of course I can do this. I'll be fine. I mean, on the day, I'll be cool. I swear I won't go nuts on him. Oh my god, he is so cute! I can't believe I get to go backstage to meet him!

My friends are going to freak when they hear this! They won't believe me! Oh! Can I bring a friend? Please? Yes? Oh my god, that is amazing. I can't wait! Oh my god!

Wait. What? One of my parents has to come? Why? Ew, no! Are you kidding? But then it won't be fun! No, that doesn't mean I don't want the passes, I do! OK, sure, my dad will come. We'll ditch him somehow later.

Oh my god, this is going to be the first day of the rest of my life!

TOO MUCH

DAISY is a truly obsessive fan. Here, she forces a meeting with the object of her affections and tries to convince him of how right they are for each other.

I love you. I mean it. I love you. I think we're supposed to be together. I know that sounds crazy; you don't even know me! But I watch your show every week, and I read everything about you. We like *all* the same things.

We're meant to be. I'm sure of it. You look like you're scared. Don't be! I'm really nice. You're going to like me.

I found out you where you live through a friend's father. Everyone knows how much I like you. I'm going to owe my friend's dad *forever*. Can I come in? Just for a little while? Give me a chance, Jeremy! Give me, like, an hour. If you don't like me after that, I'll walk away and never bother you again. But I just *know* you're going to like me. Give me a chance, Jeremy, please!

(Shouting.) I'll leave now, but I'm going to come back every day, Jeremy! I know we're meant to be together!

SIDE KICK TO THE GUT

ROBERT is the shy sidekick to the loudest kid in school.
But the act is getting old.

I don't understand you. Did you not get enough attention as
a child? How come you always have to be the center of attention? It gets really boring. I am starting to hate being
around you. It's too much . . . I don't know. Just too much.
No one ever looks at me. No one ever sees me. You make
sure of that. Why can't I ever be the one that people talk to?
Why do you always have to be so loud? God forbid anyone
actually is interested in me. You always see that it doesn't
last long.

It's not your personality. You force it. You don't have to try
so hard. Being the life of the party doesn't mean talking over
everyone and laughing the loudest. Well, maybe it does. But I
don't have to listen to it anymore! I'm sick of being your
sidekick all the time. I want to be seen, too. If you can't let
me be . . . visible, then I guess we just shouldn't be around
each other anymore.

ONE MOMENT

ANDREA wants very much to fit in with a new crowd. She is faced with a critical decision.

Are you sure you're feeling OK? I don't know, TJ. Maybe we should call someone to drive us. I'm just saying you had a lot to drink. I'm not judging you. I don't care how much you drink. That's your right. I'm just saying maybe you shouldn't drive. I know you feel OK, but maybe you're not.

What if we get into an accident? What if we get hurt or if you hurt someone else? I'm not being melodramatic! These things happen.

Lots of time. You've done this lots of times. So? *I* wasn't in the car those times. You know what, if you want to risk *your* life, fine. But don't risk mine.

So you're going to leave me here alone? You're just going to drive away? You can't! TJ! OK, fine, fine! I'll get in the car with you. Just be careful, OK?

LIFE ON MARS

JAY is a huge fan of science and science fiction. Other kids think he's a bit odd. He is very passionate and serious about his beliefs.

What is so funny? I believe in aliens. Life on other planets. What's so hilarious about that? It statistically makes sense. Why should we be the only living beings in the universe? You believe in evolution, right? So, why wouldn't there be being that adapted to hotter or colder environments than ours? And who knows what lies beyond the world we're aware of.

This is not funny. You're so ignorant. What do you believe about life on other planets then? You're not being logical. It makes sense.

No, I don't believe in, like, *Star Trek* and that kind of thing. On those shows, they have to use human actors so basically all of the aliens look like people. Why would that be true? No, I don't think aliens will look like blobs. I don't know what they'd look like. They'd look like nothing we've ever seen, dummy! They live in a completely different environment!

You guys are dorks.

THE VIDEO

AUSTIN has been a video junkie, wannabe filmmaker his whole life. But one of his past creations from his youth has returned to haunt him.

Why is everyone laughing when I walk down the hall? What's going on? Do I have a booger on my face or something?

What? A video? I didn't make a video. When I was a kid? What are you talking about?

No. No! Tell me you're kidding. I made those lip-sync videos when I was, like, ten. How did—Jeff! Oh my god, I'm going to *kill* him. Well, I was in front of the camera, but he was into being the director. Everything I did was *his* idea. He used to tell me I was a really good rapper, so I believed him. I was *ten*! Wait, so how did this get to everyone?

It was on *TV*?!!? That is not fair. He should have to get my permission. He won money? I deserve that money. That is cruel. How could he do this at my expense? *Everyone's* laughing at me. And not even just in school, I guess. I can't go in public at all now! I am going to sue Jeff. I can't believe he'd do this to me!

PUZZLE #87

ELLEN loves to challenge her mind with games and puzzles. Lately, she's become consumed with Sodoku.

You go on. I have to finish this. I can't help it; I'm addicted! Besides, you know me. Once I start something I have to finish it. I'm compulsive.

Have you ever tried these things? It's this Japanese game, where . . .

If this makes me a loser, then I guess I'm a loser. But I can't stop. It's like my drug. I see these squares in my sleep, I swear. I wake up trying to work out puzzles that I've made up in my head. How surreal is that? But I'm getting really good at it! I finished a few "diabolical" puzzles! Not all of them, and there are a few easier ones I can't get—

Just go shopping then! I have to finish this. I'm sorry, but there's no way I can stop. I'll just see you later then. Oh, could you . . . you turned that pillow upside-down. Could you fix it on your way out? Thanks!

BLIND DATE

HOWIE is strong academically, but awkward socially. He's about to meet a girl he's been talking to online for the first time. He brought along his best friend, Jeff, just in case things don't go well.

I'm so nervous. What if she's ugly? What if she has a really annoying voice? What if she never shows up? What if she thinks *I'm* ugly?

It's just that I've never seen this girl before. We've only e-mailed each other. This seemed like such a good idea. Meeting each other. Maybe this is a big mistake. Let's go. This was a bad idea. She's probably insane. She's probably a psycho killer. She's probably—

Hi! Are you . . . Inge? Hi! Oh my god. You look . . . great. And you seem so . . . normal. Oh, him? He's no one. He's going. He's just my friend, Jeff. He hates everything you like. I swear. And he's leaving! He has to go to . . . Sardinia. Bye, Jeff. Have a great trip. I *said* BYE, Jeff. Stop staring at each other! *I'm* the one who's been writing to you instead of studying or sleeping. *I'm* the one who keeps getting in trouble for blocking the phone lines! Hello? Anyone listening? I can't believe this!

HOLDING THE LINE

ANNA subscribes to her parents' strong, traditional moral values, despite peer pressure to do otherwise. She tries to explain her stance to her friend.

I don't care if everyone else is "doing it." I'm not everyone else. Why should I be? I don't get it. We're taught our whole lives to be ourselves, but when I'm myself, nobody likes it. I'm weird. Can't you accept that I'm just not like you in this way? It doesn't mean we can't be friends; I'm just not in the same place, that's all. I just don't feel comfortable with all that.

I don't know, I guess my parents have an influence on me. I know I'm supposed to be rebellious, but I just don't feel like it. I *like* my parents. They're nice. They're good to me. And I respect their opinions and values. I know that sounds corny, but it's true. Plus, there are all these downsides—pregnancy, diseases—not to mention . . . I'd feel so dirty and bad. I don't know. I'd just feel the whole time that my parents would know and that God was watching and I was going to hell and I just can't imagine . . . I don't know! I know it's not cool, but . . . can you just respect my feelings? I'm just not like that. But I still want to be your friend, OK?

HOMELESS

> *KATE comes from a very religious family. When her fa-*
> *ther finds out she is dating behind his back, he jumps to*
> *conclusions and kicks Kate out of the house.*

I don't know where to go. Can I stay with you, Matt? My
parents kicked me out. I don't know why! They're just mad
at me for not being like them, not being good enough. They
found out about us. And you know how religious my parents
are. I'm not supposed to date until I'm eighteen. So now my
dad thinks I'm a whore, and he told me to get out. I told him
that we weren't like that, I'm not like that and *you're* not
like that, but he wouldn't listen. How could they be so heart-
less? My mom did nothing, just stood there. They threw me
out on the street! They don't care about me at all, Matt.
They don't love me. I could get killed out on the street!

Are you serious? You don't think your parents will let me
stay here? Well, where am I supposed to go? I never
thought—I'm really going to be on the street! What am I
going to do? Why is God doing this to me?

TESTING 1-2-3

ERIKA has severe problems with her heart, and they've grown worse. She's waiting in the hospital to hear the results of the latest tests.

Please don't tell anyone. Your dad didn't tell anyone else, did he? I'm just in here for a little while. They're doing tests. They think . . . Well, I guess you know what they think. But it might not be. I'm hoping it's not that bad. Fingers crossed, right? So, it was nice of you to stop by to see me.

People are asking about me at school? God, that's nice. I wonder what I should tell them when I get back. I don't want anyone to know about this. I don't want people to feel sorry for me or anything.

So your dad works here? Cool. Does he know . . . anything? About me? You look like you feel bad for me. Do you know something? Where are my parents? They've been gone forever. It's true, isn't it? I can tell by your face. Oh god, Cat, I'm gonna die.

SUDDENLY SEXY

> HENRY *is a sweet, geeky kind of guy who, over the summer, got very cute and good-looking. He's not sure how to handle the attention he's getting from girls now because it's very new to him.*

Um, can I talk to you about something? Get your opinion about something? Well, I guess it's no secret that I've never exactly been popular. But the thing is, this year I started getting popular for some reason. I guess since I got taller or something? I don't know. Anyhow, this girl in my class, this really popular girl, decided I was cute or something. I don't know. I'm the same person, basically, so I don't know what that's about. So, anyway, now she thinks I'm cute. And since she thinks it, a lot of other girls do, too. It's kind of overwhelming. Do I need to pick just one? I'm not sure I want to pick one at all. I kind of like the attention, but the idea of getting serious with someone—Well, I don't know if I want that just now. And I kind of wonder sometimes if this is some kind of joke.

I was just thinking you're older and maybe you know more about this. I mean, I've never been, like, a stud or something. It's kind of weird. I mean, it's good, but it's weird. Because I'm the same person I always was. Know what I mean?

NO TECHNO

*CHARLIE has unassuming, loving parents who don't see
the point of gadgets like cell phones and MP3 players. He
commiserates with a friend.*

I am the only kid in America without a cell phone and an
iPod, aren't I? My parents are so harsh. They say I don't
need it! Of course I need it. Even if I never use them, I need
them. It's just sad being the only kid in America without
them!

Know what, though? I have to say, maybe because I've never
had a cell phone, that I don't know who I'd call and text all
the time. I really don't have that much to say. You know
those kids who are texting *all* the time? I wonder what
they're saying. Their lives must be so much more interesting
or active than mine. I mean, I guess this is what I'd end up
writing, "In math class. Learning about cosigns." How boring is that? Plus, who would I send it to after I wrote it?
Probably you or one of the other guys who are probably sitting next to me in class. Maybe we need to get out more,
broaden our circle. Just in case I do ever enter the twentieth
century someday. Then I'll have people to communicate with
and I won't just be carrying around all these useless devises.

OVERSIGHT

SAM is a top student and the class vice-president. He never dreamed that he wouldn't get into the one college he applied to.

I didn't get in. Oh my god. I didn't get in. This doesn't make any sense. What am I going to do? I can't tell my parents. You don't understand. I did something—

I didn't apply anywhere else. I took the money they gave me for application fees and spent it. And I just applied to UCLA because I was *sure* I'd get in. Why wouldn't they accept me? I get good grades. I got good scores on my SAT's. Oh my god, I am so screwed!

What am I going to do, Rob? My parents are going to kill me. And I never wanted to spend a year at home with them doing some lame-ass job. This has got to be a mistake.

Everyone else is going to be having fun going to parties and classes and meeting new people, and I'm going to be here with my parents working at the grocery store. Oh my god, my life is over, Rob. I am dead!

BEST FRIEND

GARRETT is a really nice guy and every girl's best friend. He's trying to talk some sense into a friend in a bad relationship.

I don't understand you. He's no good for you. Why do you want to go back to him? I don't want to make you mad at me, but . . . He says terrible things to you. Every time you want to eat something, he says, "Are you sure you want that?" like you're built like a truck or something. Even if you were, he shouldn't talk to you like that. If he wants a skinny girl, he should just get one instead of making you feel bad all the time. You look good, and he makes you feel bad about yourself. You know it's true.

I *know* you love him, but . . . why? What did he do to deserve you? He doesn't love you. If he loved you, he wouldn't tell you you're fat. He wouldn't talk about other girls and their bodies in front of you. He's a jerk. I'm sorry. I'm sorry. I just don't understand you right now. I'm trying to be a friend.

Fine. Fine. Never mind. Forget I said anything. Really. I'm sorry.

THE GOOD ONE

KEVIN is the kid who never gets in trouble. Why does he have to be so considerate of his brother, the family screw-up?

Why are you mad at me? I'm the good one, remember? Since when am I responsible for my older brother? I don't know where he went. He doesn't tell me anything. He's probably out with his friends drinking and injecting heroin or something. Why are you mad at me? *I'm* sitting at home doing my homework.

So I'm not supposed to say anything bad about Paul. I'm, what? Suppose to pretend he's a really swell kid? I just don't get it. You're always mad at *me*. And I'm always trying to be good! I can't help it if Paul is constantly screwing up! Why am I supposed to pretend like I don't notice? God forbid I ever say anything bad about precious Paul. I'm just telling the truth! You taught me to tell the truth. You're a real hypocrite, you know that?

See, you're mad again. Whatever. I'm going to go do my homework. I guess you'll have to sit around on pins and needles 'til the good son gets home.

SECOND BEST

AUTUMN is afraid that her best friend would rather hang out with her cool, pretty, perfect sister. After all, that's how everyone else feels.

I didn't tell you about my sister because I don't have a sister. At least I don't think of her as my sister. We're just . . . biologically attached. That's all. She's no sister to me. Look, she comes across cool at first, but she's really a huge bitch.

Fine. Go ahead. Be *her* best friend now. That's how it always goes. People meet my sister, and I disappear.

Yeah, her hair is dyed. She tells people it's not, but she's got a Clairol bottle under her desk in her room. You would not believe the stories I could tell you.

So you don't like her better? You're not just saying that? She *is* pretty vain. And we don't go to the same school because she's not as smart as me. Yeah, she's a complete loser.

Know what, Jenny? You're the best friend I ever had.

THE PRIZE

KRISTINE is a contestant on a reality show requiring a lot of physical strength and endurance. Unfortunately, her partner in this challenge is less athletic than she is.

Don't you want this? If you want this, you have to get up and get moving! Why do I feel like I'm doing this alone? There are *thousands* of dollars on the line here. You cannot give up. I won't *let* you give up. I need this money. Get up and get moving. I'm not joking. I'll carry you if I need to, but, obviously, we probably won't win that way. We have to be in this together. We're a team.

Are you trying to hurt me? Is this punishment for what I said to you yesterday?

Of course, you can breathe! Asthma is just a state of mind. You're just being weak. You can push through this. Mind over matter!

Oh my god, you really can't breathe! Why is this happening? Oh, this sucks. Hey! Can anyone hear me? We need help here!

THE BIG HOPE

RYAN is the star player on his football team with a demanding and competitive father. Unfortunately, he recently injured his knee, possibly ruining his chances for college scholarships and a professional career.

Dad, I can't help that I need a knee replacement. It's not like I chose this. Believe me, I'm not excited about this. I'm nervous. What if there's a problem? What if I can't walk, what if I can't run? I want this as much as you do. I want to go pro. So I have to have a lot more good years in me. If I'm not a football player, what am I? This is our whole life. Do don't give me a hard time about this, Dad. I'm already punishing myself about this.

It was just a second, a moment, I lost my focus. I didn't even see that guy coming from the side. I can't believe this! How can your whole life change in just a second?

This is going to work, right? God, Dad, don't make me feel like I let you down. Please. I'll do whatever work I have to do to get back in shape. I'll work on my upper body while my knee is healing. This is not going to hold me back, Dad. I'm going to make our dream come true.

BEST MAN

JAKE is a runner. For years, he was the best in his event. Recently, however, a competitor from another school keeps beating him.

Congratulations. The best man won.

I hate that guy. He's not human. Can we get him tested for steroids? He beats me every time. *Every* time! It's not right. It's not human! I train like crazy!

No, I'm not a quitter. I'll keep going. I guess I just need to work out more. Run more. Maybe I should take some supplements. If I was lighter, I'd be faster, right?

Don't worry about me. I'm fine. I feel fine. I'm healthy. I work out all the time, how could I not be? I just need to win. This is supposed to be my ticket into college. I always thought this is what I do best. It *is* what I do best. Until this guy came along. I can't be overshadowed. I have to win. I will do whatever it takes. That guy is going to be sorry he ever saw me. I am going to win. I am going to take the state title. I am going to get a scholarship into college, and will do *anything* to make that happen. No one wants this more than me. No one.

PLASTIC

LAYLA is spoiled and materialistic. Her father recently decided that she's spending too much money and wants to take her credit card away.

You cannot take my credit card away. I know what responsibility is! I get good grades in school. You always said that's my job in life at this stage. So I am doing my part. How can you punish me? It's not my fault that money is tight. You taught me to be like this. I can't help that I need clothes and stuff. Plus, don't you want me to have friends? How can I do that unless I can go out with them and eat, shop, go to the movies? Do you want me to be friendless?

No! You are joking. Not the car! You can't take my car! You *gave* me that car. I earned it for getting honor roll for a whole year. You always taught me that you can't take back what you give. Giving is selfless. So how can you be going back on everything you taught me? I don't get this! Maybe *you* should stop playing golf and going out to dinner. Maybe *you* should be the one who has to buy less. Where is this coming from? It's not like we're poor. I don't know how you can just pull this on me all of a sudden. It's not fair. I guess you don't love me. I don't know what I did that was so wrong.

This is sick. You're going to have to find another way. If you try to take my car, I'll drive away and never come back. I'm serious. Try me.

MOVING ON

SABRINA wants to move to New York City. Her parents want her to go to the local college and live at home.

I'm *not* going to school here, Mom. I refuse. I want to get away from here! I have to! I have to get out of this town and away from you and make my own life. That's what college is for.

If you won't pay for NYU, then I'll just move out and go to New York myself. I'll get a job. *That's* how I'll afford it. Just like everyone else. And if I never get to college, well, that will be all your fault. But I can't stay here. I'll die. Everyone knows me and my whole history. I need a new start. I need to meet people who are more like me. I need a chance to become something. I can't do that here.

Look, I got into a great school! Why can't you and Daddy be happy for me?

I don't have to do what you say anymore. If you won't support me, I'll just pack my bags and leave now. Is that what you want? I'll do it! I'm serious! Don't tempt me.

POWERS

JOEY is fascinated with the occult and very superstitious. Recently, he's started believing that he has magical powers and is confessing his thoughts for the first time to a friend.

I think I'm a witch or a warlock or whatever. I think I have . . . powers. No, it's possible. I think . . . I think I can move things with my mind. Seriously! I'm not pretending! Don't be stupid. I have not been watching those Harry Potter films. This is an actual thing! Look, I'm telling you this because I thought I could confide in you. I thought you, of all people, would believe me. Don't you think it's possible, in the entire realm of things that could happen in the universe, that I could be sort of . . . magical? Why not! Come on, Dan, I am depending on you here for a little support!

You're not supposed to doubt. You're supposed to believe. That's how magic works. But fine. I'll show you. I'll move that candle on my dresser.

(Concentrates.) I can't focus. It's your negativity. I could do it yesterday, I swear. No, I'm not "on" anything! God! People are so prejudiced against my kind. It's not fair.

WHO I AM

MAURA doesn't feel comfortable in her own skin. She recently saw a counselor and discovered that she is not alone or abnormal. But now she has to explain to her mother that Maura wants to be Mark.

Mom, I have to tell you something that's going to make you mad. Please don't be. I just have to tell someone. I have to tell you. Now it's not like I've *done* anything. I just have to say something about me, about who I am. Wow, this is hard. I want to be a boy. I've always wanted to be a boy. Ever since I was little. I guess it's no secret the way I hate to wear dresses and that kind of stuff. But until recently, I don't know, I didn't think it was possible to become a boy. I just didn't see how everything could . . . work, but I was talking to someone—

Don't get mad, Mom. This isn't something I can help. That's what I learned. This is just—Some people are born like this. But, see, Mom, this is really a good thing! I can be fixed. There's, like, a way for me to feel normal. I just have to take hormones and get an oper—

I don't know how I'll get the money. I just know I have to do it. I want you to support me on this. I feel like it's something I have to do. I have to, or I'll die! Please, Mom! Don't walk away from me!

THE STAND

TINSLEY is hard working, artistic, and sensitive, but she feels like she doesn't measure up in her parent's eyes.

No matter what I do, you're never happy! What do you want from me? Is there anything in this whole universe I can do that will please you? I'm not a robot, you know. I'm just so sick of trying to be perfect all the time! It's impossible! So why do I bother?

You have no idea what you've got. It could be so much worse. I know kids in my class who are on drugs and drink all the time, and get *really* bad grades, not B's, and they are having sex with anything that moves. I am a good kid! Why can't you see that? I can't help that I'm ordinary. Not everyone can be perfect like you, Dad. Some of us are just doing the best we can, and we're not totally brilliant. Maybe I won't be rich and brilliant like you. Is that the worst thing in the world?

Know what? I don't want to be you. I want to be *me.* And I like wearing baggy clothes and listening to music and playing guitar. I'm sorry that's not good enough for you, but screw you if you don't like it! I'm not going to try to be what you want anymore!

DEGREES OF NORMAL

JUNE is awkward, smart, funny, and intense. Lately, June has been frustrated at the unfair standards of beauty she sees all around her.

What is it about me? I'm not disgusting or anything, am I? I mean, in the grand scheme of things, is there anything so awful about me? I have all of my limbs, I have all the right parts in generally the right places. So what's my problem? Why do people find me so repellent? Specifically, why do males find me so disgusting? I know I'm not skinny or really pretty. I'm just normal. But what's so bad about that? Not every guy is gorgeous. In fact, very few are. And most of them are too stupid and full of themselves for my taste. So I'm not even looking at *them*. I just want a regular guy. Just a normal, decent, honest human being. But, apparently, that's impossible. Because I'm disgusting. Because I'm not a model or something. It's not fair. Why does every guy think he can and should get a hot babe? Where does that leave the rest of us? Ugly guys think they should get hot girls. It's crazy. I just can't be beautiful and perfect. I hate it, but it's true. Sometimes I think I'm above all this beauty stuff and the pressure to be perfect from TV and magazines and all that, and other times what I want most in the world is to be beautiful, so I don't have to think about this shit anymore.

I hate myself. What is it about me that makes me so unlovable?

LOATHING

BILL is suicidal and lonely. His sister, Lacey, wants desperately to save him, but he is lost in his own despair.

Leave me alone, Lacey. You don't understand. Nobody does. You have hope. You have the possibility of a normal life. People accept you just as you are, and you don't have to apologize for who you are or what you feel. You don't have to keep secrets and be ashamed. I'm an abomination. I'm disgusting. I hate myself. Do you know what it feels like to think that you are destined to be alone for the rest of your life? That you are always going to be hated? That people can't even stand looking at you? No one in my whole life will ever love me. Sure, people feel sorry for me sometimes. But pity is not love, and no one can love me. Just think about that for a minute. You will never have to feel this hopeless and empty. You can't even imagine how bad this is. So leave me be. Let me do what I have to do. I'm sitting here in the garage for a reason, OK? This is the one peaceful thing I can do for myself. I want to be free of this life and this body. I want to sit in my car and just wait to die. If God is as good as people say, maybe the next life will be better than this one. It can't be any worse.

RAVE OR RAGE

SARAH is a huge party girl whose parents try to control her by giving her a curfew. This time, she's extremely late.

What time is it? Oh my god, I was hoping my watch was wrong! I am in such trouble. I was supposed to be home two hours ago! I'm afraid to even look at my phone. Oh god, six messages. They think I'm dead, so when I get home, they are going to kill me. I didn't even hear it ring! I am not going to be able to go to a party again for the next twelve years. What am I gonna do? I can't call them because they'll freak out. But they're probably worried and freaking out, and I don't want them to think something's happened.

I can't text them. They just have a regular phone. They live in the ice age. Come with me! Say we got a flat tire! We can just throw the spare somewhere so they'll never know it's not true. But why didn't I call? Why didn't I call? A dead spot? No reception? Would that work?

Maybe they need to see that I can stay out later and be fine. Maybe this is good for them! Who am I kidding? I'm going to be killed!

THE MISTAKE

LIA is obsessed with everything being "right." She recently made a really poor, stupid decision because she wanted to be the perfect girlfriend.

Can we talk for a second? I had . . . I did something . . . bad. I did something I shouldn't do. That I didn't want to do. That—well, not exactly didn't want to—well, yes, didn't want to. I mean, I didn't like . . . I had sex with someone. Someone else. Well, obviously. It's just that . . . don't be like that. Don't be upset. I know you can't help it, but you need to hear why. You need to know. I did it because I love you. And I want everything to be right and good between us.

That *does* make sense! It *does*! Think about it. I'm just so worried . . . I want things to be right with us. I don't want to be scared. I don't want you to hate me because I'm not good enough or something. So . . . that's why I did it. Please, please, don't be upset with me. Please! I mean, I know it was wrong, but I did it for you. I wasn't even going to tell you, but I have to be honest with you. I had to tell you. But you have to understand that it didn't mean anything, and I love *you*. Please, don't be mad at me. Please? I can't be without you. *You're* the one I love. Please?

TABLE FOR THREE

BEN doesn't have his license yet, so his dad is his ride to the movies, etc. Trouble is, Ben likes things just so and his dad is the complete opposite—a joker. And the problem is just getting worse . . .

Dad, you're cramping my style. I'm older now, and I really don't want you going on dates with me. I know you have to pick me up, but this is beyond . . . A date is for *two* people! This was the worst date of my life! It's bad enough that you have to drive me; you can't come along *on* the date, too! You just kept saying how you *love* horror movies—Don't you know why people go to horror movies on a date? She girl is supposed to scream and grab my hand—You ruined it, Dad!

Don't *talk* to my dates. You need to be invisible. Obviously, I need you at this point because I can't get places on my own, but . . . you're just being too . . . friendly and nice and, well, *there.*

No, no! You're taking this all wrong. This is why I didn't want to tell you. But I had to! You're ruining my social life!

THE RIGHT GUY

NETTIE is one of those people best described as "well rounded." She seems to excel at everything she does. Except for dating. She just can't seem to attract the right guy.

This is an awful thing to say, but I don't think I could go out with Mike. Yeah, he's cute. But the thing is . . . I'm going to sound like such a snob, but he's . . . not very smart. I'm too picky; I know! But I deserve a smart guy, don't I? I'm smart, and I want someone I can talk to! I know he's nice, but . . . maybe you should go out with him. He really likes me? I don't know why. Part of me wants to say yes, I mean, I'd have a boyfriend and that would be a real load off of my mind, especially with prom coming up. But I want the *right* guy. No, I don't have someone else in mind. Not exactly. I mean, not anyone who'd actually *go* with me.

Never mind! I never said anything. Forget it, Jeannie! I was just blabbing. OK! OK! There is . . . someone. But I don't want to talk about it. You'll laugh at me. Promise you won't? Promise? I mean it. You'd better not if I tell you. OK.

No! Never mind! I can't say it! It's hopeless! Oh, Jeannie, I just can't go out with Mike. He's just not "it" for me.

Don't press me anymore! I won't tell you!

FULL

EMMA has eating disorder issues; she is consumed with controlling her food intake. She just got back home from being hospitalized with anorexia and feels her family members are scrutinizing her and judging her.

I'm not hungry, OK? Is that OK with everyone? I swear, I can't stand the way you all watch me like a hawk. It's like I'm a zoo exhibit or something. Let's watch this weird female human species! What will she eat? How much? Ever since I've gotten back from the hospital, you're all acting so obnoxious! I just want to be normal now. I want to be treated like a regular person. I'm OK! I feel fine! I'm eating. I am! But you need to trust me a little. I'm not hungry now, and if you make me eat, I'll puke it up. Because I'm *full* not because I'm bulimic! Don't jump to conclusions, OK? It's really insulting. Give me a little credit. I can't stand being judged and monitored by you all the time. I need some privacy. I don't want you listening at the door when I go in the bathroom.

Do you know Americans are pigs? We're the fattest people in the world. Our portions are too big. These are facts. So don't freak out if I don't want to eat every stupid thing on my plate! I'm doing my best, and I'd do even better if you all would just leave me alone!

BETRAYAL

PETE *recently hooked up with his best friend's girlfriend.*

I'm sorry, man. It just happened. We were drinking, it was dark, she was upset . . . It wasn't planned. And she said you were breaking up. Honestly, I didn't know what I was doing. She came onto me! I was just . . . going with the flow. I didn't mean anything by it. Come on, you can't be mad about what we did when we were drunk. We were drunk! We didn't know what we were doing.

I'm not into her, honestly, man. It was just the moment; know what I mean? Look, what do you want me to say? Yeah, she's attractive, but I'm just not into her. Really. I'm sorry, man, I really am. Can't we just forget all about this? It didn't mean anything. Do you want to ruin a friendship over this? You're like a brother to me. I would never do anything *intentionally*—Listen, man, you can have her. I don't want her. I swear. I like to keep my options open.

I GOT IT

ZACK is ladies' man. But today, his act doesn't go as well as expected.

You look beautiful. I mean it. Really good. I like that dress. You look *nice*. So . . . what do you think of me? I look good, right? What? I am not vain. Well, maybe I am, but not without reason, right? Why do you have to be so hard? You got a problem or something? I'm just trying to give you a compliment. When did that become a federal offense? OK, fine. I'll back off. I was just trying to be nice, know what I mean? My mother taught me to give a lady a compliment. I was just being real, you know? But if you have a problem with that, that's cool. It's fine. I'll just go . . . if you're sure that's what you want. I'm just giving you another chance to experience me. 'Cause I *am* an experience. Think again. I'll give you another shot at me. Take a good look before you say anything.

Hey, where you going? I was too much for you, wasn't I? You can't handle me. Don't feel bad. Very few women can! *(Yelling.)* If you change your mind, I'll be over here! Hanging out! See you later, baby!

THE BREAK UP

TAYLOR is the most popular guy in school. He is dating the most popular girl in school. That is, until today.

You're what? *You're* breaking up with *me*? But I'm the one that should leave. This isn't fair! I've been thinking about breaking up with you for weeks. *I'm* the one who hasn't been having fun for ages. Just yesterday I was thinking, "If I have to walk around the mall aimlessly with her one more time . . . " How can you possibly be breaking up with *me*?

I'm too good for you. It's so obvious. Everyone sees it! And *you* are walking away from me? No one will believe it. There are loads of other girls who are dying for a chance at me.

Don't do this. Please? I don't want us to break up. I really don't. We were so good together. Let's give it another try. Please? Just give me one more chance. Please??

Oh, that's great. I gotta go now. But first, I have something to tell you. We're over. Bye!

EMERGENCY REPAIR

MIA is inspecting her friend Cassie's wardrobe choice. It is found wanting.

No, no, no, no, no. You can't wear that. You can't! I can't be seen with you if you're wearing that. Go change. I'm not joking. You need to put on something else now.

That looks so . . . ugly. It looks like you bought it at K-Mart. It's so last year and not in a retro way. It's disgusting. I'm sorry if I'm being a bitch, but I'm just trying to help. I have your best interests at heart. I'm just telling you this because I love you.

Don't get upset, Cassie! Fashion is not about having a lot of money. I'm not making fun of you because you don't shop at Barneys. You just need to know how to put things together better. Don't worry. I'll help you. You're going to be OK. Just leave everything up to me. You'll look like a supermodel in no time. I swear!

SECRET

DAVE is fun, well liked, and gay. His current boyfriend is still in the closet, and Dave doesn't want to keep their relationship a secret anymore.

I can't do this anymore. You are just too in denial. And, frankly, I don't get it. This isn't a big deal. You're gay—so what? *Sorry. Excuse me.* God forbid anyone actually heard me say that! Well, I just can't be with someone who's ashamed of who he is. I have too much self-esteem for that.

You need to face the facts. You are *gay*. Right, right. You like *girls*. You're just *confused*. Whatever. Denial is not just a river in Egypt. Well, don't worry. I wasn't in love with you or anything. At least not yet. It's just a shame. You *are* cute. One day you'll be sorry you let me slip through your fingers.

Listen, what aren't you getting here? *I'm* the one calling it off here. Fine, fine! I won't say anything. Just calm down. Jesus.

AFTER

SEELA is a member of the in crowd but still feels like she's on the outside and has to work to keep her social status. She recently lost her virginity and is not feeling very positive about this experience.

Britt, Jace and I had sex. Last night. I don't know, I guess it was OK. Well, to be honest . . . The real truth is that I hated it. It was horrible. Totally embarrassing and painful and humiliating and not fun. I'm really worried. I'm worried there's something wrong with me. I'm supposed to like sex. This is supposed to be an amazing thing. And I don't care if I ever do it again. It was that bad. What's wrong with me? I wish I knew why I was this way. Everyone else thinks it's great, obviously. I thought this was going to be so great. I finally have a boyfriend who's really amazing, and I finally thought I'd feel like everyone else. I thought I'd feel different. Like, privileged or popular or special or something. But I just feel like a freak. And what am I going to do about Jace? What am I supposed to tell him? My whole life is falling apart, Brittney!

QUITTER

CORAL is a cheerleader with all the perks and benefits that go with that post. Even though her life looks rosy on the outside, inside the stress is really getting to her.

Jamie, can I tell you a secret? Promise you won't tell anyone? I don't want to be a cheerleader anymore. The pressure is too much. So I think when I go to college, I'll just stop. I won't go to tryouts.

My mom will definitely disown me if she finds out. And all the coaches will be so disappointed that after they worked so hard to help me get better, I just gave up. But I'm serious. I can't take it anymore. My leg kills me all the time. I tried not to talk about it in practice, but it really hurts all the time.

I don't know what it's going to be like, not being a cheerleader. It's been my identity ever since I can remember. I like being a part of something and the excitement of being in front of a crowd. I'll miss that. But I think I'm just going to go completely mental if I don't stop doing this now.

DON'T TELL

GINA is secretly dating a guy who's not cool. She doesn't want her friends to know about him.

No, he's a dork. I'm totally not interested in him. No way! Stop! Shut up about it. You're being stupid. I DON'T LIKE HIM.

(Gina notices Will.) Oh. Hi, Will. *(Gina moves away from her friends to speak to him.)* What's the matter? You're acting weird. Oh. That. No, I wasn't talking about you. I was talking about someone else. Really! Why don't you believe me? I don't think you're a dork. I mean, I like you. I do. I would never say bad things behind your back.

I don't know. I just don't want people to know about us. I like it being just us. Don't you like that? I like that it's, like, our secret. The two of us against the world.

I'm not ashamed of you! What do you want me to say? I told you I like you. Look, I can't! I just can't tell people about us. I don't want to. Why can't you respect what I want? Please, don't walk away. Look, Will, I don't know what to do here! Can't we just stay like we are?

DON'T ASK ME

ISAIAH *is trying to act like a gangsta/player to impress a girl.*

(With loads of attitude.) Yo, yo, baby, what up? You are lookin' fine. How 'bout you and me—

(Dropping the act.) What? No, I don't want to dance. I'm a guy. Guys don't dance. *(Back in character.)* You lovely, bootilicious—

(Real again.) Yeah, I know I'm black. Of course, I know that. Do I look like a fool? Just because I'm black doesn't mean I can dance. Next you're going to tell me that I ought to be able to play basketball. Well, I can't, before you ask.

So, what? You only go out with ballerinas or something?

Well, sure, I have rhythm. That has nothing to do with . . . I just don't want to . . . look . . . silly. I have to protect my image as a, um, you know. A ladies' man. *(Yelling.)* So can I get your number?

RELAX

MICHAEL's mother catches him smoking pot and is really concerned.

Listen. People have been smoking pot for years, Mom. It really can't be that bad. They even give it to people with cancer and stuff. Now why would they do that if it kills you? Mom, Mom, Mom, you're not making sense. People die from, like, heroin and crack and stuff. The idea that pot is as bad as, say, heroin, is crazy. They are completely different. Think about it; think about it. Pot just makes you calm. When I smoke pot, I just want to relax. What's dangerous about that? So it's really not that bad. Let's keep this in perspective.

Come on! I am not addicted. It's not a problem. I can stop, it's just that I don't think it's that bad. They give it to sick people, Mom! Think about it!

You cannot send me to rehab for pot. The people there will just laugh at me. There are people at those places with *real* problems. Come on! Think about it! This is too extreme! OK, what if I promise not to do it again? Mom, this is way out of proportion! The punishment does not fit the crime! Now I'm going to be "that kid who went to rehab" at school. This is insane! I can't believe you're overreacting like this.

CONTRACTING

SEAN is responsible and mature, but his father's illness is really worrying him. Normally, he would not let it show, but as his father's condition deteriorates, he feels the need to express how he feels.

He's on a feeding tube. I feel terrible. I can't even look at him. I don't know what to do. I want to *do* something for him. I don't know what I'm going to do without my dad. If he . . . This is crazy. It's so unfair. Other people don't get along with their dads, but my dad is the best. He's my life. We're, like, the same person. Why should he be the one who—I just never thought it would get this far. I always thought he'd get better. He said he would. He promised. And I believed him. I don't know what to say to him! Part of me is so mad at him. He *promised* . . . And, of course, I know that sounds stupid. Everyone dies. And he can't stop it from happening. I mean, he tried. Except . . . I heard he and my mom talking a while back about how he didn't want to go through chemo again. Why? Why can't he keep fighting? It's like he gave up. He's leaving me. And it's not fair. I don't want him to go. I don't want not to see him. But I'm just so mad! And sad. And—

I can't deal with this. I don't know what to think or do. Everything is wrong.

FIRE AT 207 NORTH STREET

EVE's house in on fire and her little sister is missing.

Where's Jamie? Where's Jamie! She left with us, right? She was right here! Where did she go? I have to go back! I have to find her!

(Shouting.) Jamie! Where are you? Oh my god, Mom, I had her right here. She was right here!

Mister, mister, I have to get back in that house! My sister's missing! Well, somebody has to go back in. There's a little girl who might be in there. I don't know where she went. She was right here! Oh god, I hope she's not in there. Oh god, if she dies in the fire, it's all my fault! I'm sorry, Mommy! I'm sorry! It's all my fault! I was supposed to watch her. Please, mister, can't somebody go inside? I'll go. I have to go. Please!

Jamie! Where were you? Oh my god, I was so worried about you! Don't leave me again! Stay right here! Don't you ever *ever* leave again!

STILLNESS

OWEN's parents are moving. But he doesn't want to go and leave his life and his friends behind him. He's determined to find a way to stay.

I'm not moving. You can go without me. I'm telling you, I won't go. I know I can't stay in this house! Duh. I'm not an idiot. I'll stay with my friends. Yes, for the rest of my life! Well, until I'm eighteen. Then I can just live on my own. Their parents won't care! *They* like me, unlike you guys! How come no one ever asked me if I wanted to move? How come I had nothing to do with this decision? This is my life, too! You never think of me. I just some dumb kid who walks around your house and eats your food. Well, if I'm such a pain, then you won't mind getting rid of me. Of course it's legal not to live with your parents! Otherwise orphans would be breaking the law. Just let me stay here. I'll be fine. I just want to finish high school here with all my friends. I don't want to start over. It's not fair. I'm just getting adjusted and now you want me to move. You don't care about me at all!

I'm not going! I don't care what you say. I'll find a way to stay.

DON'T EAT THE ENTREES

DRAKE hates his job, and he's on a mission to get fired.

Know what? I want to get fired from this job. It sucks! I've been trying for weeks now, and I just can't get Jeremy to fire me! My dad won't let me quit. I've *begged* him. He's really into this "a quitter never wins, and a winner never quits" crap. In my opinion, a winner quits if he's doing a sucky job. It's not like this is like being the president of the United States. We flip burgers! Personally, I don't think there's any shame in quitting something that doesn't even matter in the grand scheme of things. It's not like someone's going to die if I don't flip burgers. This kind of crap food kills people, so I'd probably be doing the world a favor if I quit. But my dad just won't hear it. What if, like, Einstein was doing this job and wouldn't quit? Then we wouldn't have that theory of relativity, whatever that does for the world. I just know it's important.

So, anyway, I've tried being obnoxious and lazy and giving people the wrong orders and setting off the fire alarms. Today I think I'll pull out the big guns. I just wanted to warn you. Get your lunch from the food court today because I am going to spit in everything!

THE TROUBLE WITH TAFFETA

LAUREN is independent and individualistic. She has no desire to take part in the typical teenage rituals like the prom. Her mother, on the other hand, thinks she'll look back and be sorry she didn't go later in life.

The prom is such a waste, Mom. How do you know I'll regret it? I don't think I will. It's just a bunch of idiots grinding against each other in cheap satin dresses and polyester suits. With *really* bad, cheesy music playing in the background. What's good about that? What's so seminal and important that I'm going to miss? Do you think I'm going to be prom queen? News flash, Mom. I'm not going to be prom queen. I'm not one of the beautiful people. I'm not one of the popular girls. And I never could be. Besides, those girls are backstabbing bitches anyway.

That is so offensive, Mom. I am *not* jealous of them. I can't believe you said that. That is blatantly untrue. I can't *believe* you said that! Just because you aspire to that crap doesn't mean I do. I feel sorry for kids like you.

You have to face it, Mom. I'm your kid. You were a loser, and so am I.

GRAVITY

HARPER's father was never there for her when she was younger. Now he suddenly wants to be part of her life.

This is pathetic. You think you can just walk in here and be my best friend? You think just because you show up every once in a while I'm supposed to be grateful? That I'm supposed to love you just because you supplied the sperm that put me into existence? What about all the times you weren't around, Dad? Birthdays, Christmases, school events—there are so many times when I want you there, and you were nowhere to be found. That hurt me. That hurt me a lot when I was little. But now that I'm older, I don't need you. I have friends I can rely on. I have a boyfriend. He's going to take care of me. So I don't need you.

I don't know why you bothered to come here today. Why you made time out of your *busy* schedule for Gillian and me. You know, it would be better for Gillian if you just got out of our life for good. So she won't sit around waiting for you the way I did. Maybe her heart will be broken now, today, but that's better than it being broken a thousand times over like you did to me. I hate you, Dad. I mean that. I *hate* you. Why don't you go home to your other family and just leave us alone once and for all?

QUEEN NARINDA

NARINDA has a powerful personality and refuses to be pushed around. When a cheerleader tries to intimidate her at her new school, Narinda goes on the attack.

Shut up. I don't want to hear anything come out of your mouth. What did I say? I think you have the impression that I am going to take your crap. I don't take crap from anyone, especially a cheerleader. So you can stuff it, sunshine.

You seem to think that I care what you think. I don't. Everyone else in this school seems to be under the impression that you are somebody, but I'm not. I see you twenty years from now with two husbands, two divorces, desperate, doing plastic surgery after plastic surgery to recover your lost youth, living off your alimony, having no intelligence or job skills, eating a bag of Doritos while you watch soap operas. You are a sad person. So you can stop telling me what to do. Step back, sister. You do *not* want to start anything with me.

I may be the new girl, but there's a new regime coming. Your reign is over, sunshine. The queen is dead.

TOTALLY ADORABLE

AMY *is completely crazy about her first boyfriend, Robbie.*

I miss you when you're not around. Is that silly? I do. I hate that we're a whole grade apart, and I never see you in my classes. But it's probably for the best. I probably couldn't sit next to you in class without wanting to touch you. It would kill me. Can you imagine if we started making out in the middle of English class or something? That would be hysterical.

I can't concentrate on anything, you know. I think about you all the time. My grades are getting worse and worse. But I can't help it. You're so perfect. Do you feel the same way about me?

How much do you like me, Robbie? "A lot"? How much is "a lot"? Do you think maybe . . . I think maybe I'm . . . I don't know. I just like you so much. I think I might be . . . I don't know . . . I think I might maybe be falling in love with you. I don't know. I've never been in love before, so I might be wrong. It's just that—

You feel the same way? Oh, Robbie, I love you so much!

UNREQUITED

*MARY is in love with her best friend, Kel. They will soon
be attending different colleges, and Mary is trying to get
her courage up to tell Kel how she feels. Or, even better,
she wants Kel to tell her how he feels about her.*

You're my very best friend in the whole world, you know
that? I can't imagine being without you. Why do we have to
go to different colleges? It's awful. I can't imagine even having a day without you.

I sound so melodramatic, don't I? The worst part is that I
mean it. I do. You're my best friend ever, Kel. You're the
only person I can talk to. I don't want to go away to school.
I've begged my parents over and over to let me go to college
here, but they won't let me. They say it's good for me; it's
part of growing up. They don't understand.

But you'll be fine, right? You don't . . . Do you feel like that
about me? I know you don't. I know you'll be fine without
me. But you'll write me, won't you? Please? I know you're
terrible about e-mailing, but I'm your best friend, Kel. I wish
. . . I wish . . . You just mean the world to me. I'm going to
miss you so much.

HOOKED

JACE is cute and popular. For the first time in his life, he feels like he might really be in love.

I can't believe I'm saying this. I can't believe I'm even thinking this. This is so embarrassing. Promise you won't bust on me, man. I think I might be in . . . love, I guess. With Seela. I just kind of think about her all the time. She makes me feel, like, happy. I smile when I think about her. And we have so much fun together. I guess I shouldn't say it out loud or whatever. Sounds stupid to say it out loud. But how do you know you're in love or whatever anyway? I mean, what is really liking someone or even lust, and what is being in love? I've never felt like this before, so I'm not even sure what to call it. I just feel so jumpy and crazy inside. It's an awesome feeling. I just know . . . I really like her. Listen, don't tell anyone else about this. I haven't even told Seela. I don't know if I should. I don't know if it makes me seem stupid or desperate or anything. It's just that . . . I feel great, man. I hope I feel like this forever.

CLOSE TO YOU

CAT is extremely book-smart but lacks common sense.
She's planning a trip to go meet someone she met online.

If I tell you something, will you promise not to tell anyone else? Yesterday, I booked a ticket on the Internet to go to California. If my parents found out, they would absolutely go berserk. I just know I have to meet this Internet guy. We've been e-mailing each other for months and months, and I feel like I know him better than anyone I've ever met. We're just so *right* for each other.

I can't believe you are doing this. You sound just like my parents. Do you know they're checking all my emails and calls now? It's like living in a police state. It's like Big Brother. They don't give me any credit for being an intelligent person. I get straight A's in school. I'm not stupid. I know what I'm doing. This guy is awesome. I'm a really good judge of character. I picked you as a friend, right?

So how can you think it's wrong? Can't anybody trust me? I'm going to California. You'll see. It will be great. We'll get married, and my life will be perfect. I don't care what anyone thinks. I know this is right.

GET REEL

SYLVIA is a supreme romantic, though she's in complete denial about it.

God, I wish life was like the movies. I wish some guy would die for me. Can you imagine a guy waiting in the rain for you? The guys I date are always late. It's so rude. Men today have no consideration, no sense of romance. I asked my mom the other day if it gets better when they get older, and she said no. She said it gets worse.

Have you ever wanted to surf? I have. It looks so cool, but then I'm afraid that I'd drown or get bitten by a shark. But then maybe some lifeguard would save me. And that would be *awesome*. I'd love to be rescued. And I'd love him to come to the hospital to check on how I am and bring me flowers. I am not a romantic! I just like to daydream. I'm a realist. I know it's impossible. But I *do* like to wish.

VIEW FROM THE COUCH

*WILL just can't manage to care or take a stand about
anything, no matter how hard he tries. He feels guilty
about it, but, you know, what can you do?*

It's hard to be a nice person. I don't know how other people
do it. I *want* to be good. I want to go to rallies and have
causes and rage against the machine and all that, but . . . I
don't know. Then reality sets in. Old people have tubes coming out of them when they're sick. And there's this old people
smell. I can't help it. I don't like it. I know, that's a terrible
thing to say, but everybody knows it's true.

And I *really* want to be, like, politically aware, I guess, but it
just takes a lot of work. I find it all really confusing. And it's
. . . boring. That's the real truth of it. I swear, I try to watch
CNN, but then I end up looking at the other TV selections,
and there's always a show with cop chases or bloopers on. I
admit it! I can't say no to bloopers! They're hilarious! Plus,
with recycling, I have to walk *outside* to throw out my cans
and bottles. *Outside!* I don't know why we don't just keep
extra trash cans inside like normal people. But I can't be expected to recycle under those conditions! It rains sometimes!
Who wants to go out in the rain just to throw out a can? I
know it's, like, saving the earth and all, but still! So, I guess
I'm just not a good person.

COMBAT

GAVIN isn't quite an achiever at school. His father would like him to go into the army after high school so he can learn responsibility and discipline. But Gavin can't help but think of the consequences of choosing this path.

What do you think about going into the army after high school? My dad really wants me to. I don't mind the discipline and all that. My dad's that way anyhow. If I stay home after high school, I'll just have to do some stupid job like pump gas or something. My grades aren't good enough for college. One major plus is that if I went into the army I wouldn't have to hear my dad talk about how lazy I am all the time and how I need to "buckle down" and all that crap. But—

There are just so many stories about guys dying. My dad would be thrilled probably if I died in the line of duty. Isn't that sick? It would probably be the best thing I ever did in his book. But I guess I'm a coward or unpatriotic or something. I don't want to die like that.

Who am I kidding? I'm going to go. My dad's going to make me. So what's the use of talking about it?

HAIRNETS AND A SMILE

MYLES doesn't want to get a summer job. His father has other ideas and intends to get his way.

Yes, I went to the mall and filled out applications. All the jobs were filled. I did my best. There just aren't any jobs. I *did* try. Come on, do I have to do this every day? Dad, why can't I just relax for a while? School *just* ended, can't I have a few weeks to take it easy? I'll start work; I just want a little time off. Why can't I have that? This is supposed to be a vacation. Ever heard of those? I'm not being sarcastic! I'm just asking you a question. I don't think you've ever heard of a vacation. It can be good for you to take some time off to think and regroup. I'd like that.

No! I am not going to work at McDonald's! That's humiliating. I am not doing any job that involves a hat or a hairnet. No way. I promise I'll go to the mall and fill out more application tomorrow, OK? Happy?

THE PAST IS PAST

BRENDA *is an average student with a very cool persona. She is smart, but not at all into school.*

I hate history. I don't know why we have to learn this stuff. Think about what history is: stuff that happened in the past. The past is the past, right? It's *over*. Let's focus on the here and now. What do you mean, "Who is the vice president?" I don't know. That doesn't matter either. Because it doesn't *affect* me! What matters is my friends and my family and things like that. Not the government.

I hate it when people say things like that. Maybe I *won't* understand when I'm older. Maybe it doesn't matter. Maybe I'm old enough now. It's so condescending. I'm never going to think any differently. I'm never going to care who's the president and what's going on in Asia and stuff. Why should that matter? I really don't get it. I think politics and history are stupid. I don't see why I have to study this stuff. It's so pointless.

THE SYSTEM

RORY has his own system of organization, which looks like a total mess to everyone else in the world, especially his mother.

But I need all this stuff, Mom! Everything here is important. It all has a place. It's organized; you just don't know how I organize it. I can find everything in here. If you moved it, I wouldn't know where anything was.

No, I can't throw anything out! That's my bottle collection! Aren't you listening? *Everything* in here is *important*. Look, I'm not crapping up your precious dining room or anything, so what do you care if my room is a mess?

I *am* becoming an adult! So I'm asking you to respect what I want. I want a messy room. Sure, yeah. When I'm forty and married my room will probably still look like this. So? My wife won't mind. She's a slob, too. She thinks this room smells *great*. Look, Mom, if you don't come in here, you won't be upset by this mess. Then both of us will be happy.

BLACK BELT BETTY

ELIZABETH, not the most coordinated girl in the world, is attending her first karate class.

Oh! I'm so sorry! Are you OK? You told me to kick! I don't have very good aim. I'm so sorry. I mean, that's why I'm here. I'm not very athletic. Believe me, I'd never do that on purpose. I know how much that hurts, believe me.

I can't believe this. I kicked my karate instructor in the groin. This can't be good. I really didn't mean it. I thought . . . I don't know . . . I thought you'd sort of protect yourself. I guess I didn't seem like a threat, did I? Just some skinny girl. I don't blame you for not expecting me to do any damage.

I didn't do any damage, did I? You can't speak. You're in pain. You want me to get someone?

OK. I'll shut up now. You're not going to kill me or anything, are you? I really didn't mean it!

PRISONER

WENDY *is a teenage mom who wants to start dating again. Her mother disapproves and wants her to stay home with the baby. Wendy sees this as punishment for the one big mistake of her life.*

Why can't you trust me anymore? I screwed up *once*. OK, it was a big mistake, but it was *once*, Mom. I just want to go out. It's just a date. A *first* date. I haven't had a date in ages. Why can't I go? Do you really think I'd go out and get pregnant again? Give me a little credit. I don't want another baby.

I *know* I have a baby. I *know* I have to take responsibility for my actions. This isn't news. And I do all that. I take care of my baby. I never go anywhere. I never do anything. I still get good grades in school. I *am* grateful that you take care of him when I'm at school, and I *know*, since you've told me a million times, that *you* didn't want to take care of kids anymore. *You* already did that. I get it. I'm grateful. I am! I just—I want one night—just a few hours!—to be a teenager again. Joey is really nice, Mom. You'll like him. Please! I already told him I can go. Please, Mom, just give me two hours! Do I have to be punished forever for that one mistake?

You are so cruel! I hate you! I hate my whole life!

GIRLIE GIRL

NANCY is every guy's best friend, laid back and fun. In an effort to get her crush to see her as more than "one of the guys," she's ditched her casual look for something a little more . . . uncomfortable.

If this is what it's like being a girl, maybe I don't want to be a girl. You know what I mean? Not a girlie girl. High heels are unnatural. If we were supposed to be like this, our feet would grow this way. We would have evolved to have these huge, pointy heels. This is one of those things men made up to torture women. It's killing me!

Are you sure this will attract Brad, my one true love? It will be worth it if he actually looks at me for once. Well, sure he looks at me, but he doesn't *look* at me. Not in *that* way. He thinks I'm a buddy; I'm one of the guys. It's, like, my curse. I'm invisible to the opposite sex. I have no feminine charms. Zero. Ow! My ankle! This sucks!

I hate being a female. Why can't I just be me?

Brad looked at me? When? When? When I twisted my ankle? Great! Great! So he saw me looking like an ass. Fantastic. I was better off in my flip-flops!

LESS

LINDA has a reputation for being a slut. She's decided not to fight it, sometimes even building up her "bad girl" image.

So what if I have a "bad" reputation? What do I care? Know what? I like it. I like having a bad reputation. I don't have to worry about it getting worse or what other people think of me. I know what they think of me. And the kids at school are a bunch of little losers anyway, so who cares? I'm doing life research. That's how I see it. I'm trying everything. I've got an adventurous spirit. And that just happens to include sex and drugs. So what? I'm not stupid, though. I'm not going to catch anything or OD or whatever. So you don't have to worry I have cooties, buddy.

You look so nervous! Look, you either want this or not. Whatever. Let me know. I'm around.

Excuse me? Of course I have self-respect. That's so insulting! Oooh. I get it. You're a Bible boy. You're trying to save me from myself. Well, guess what? It's not possible. I'm past saving, and I don't care.

BEGINNING

CONNOR *is an ex-delinquent just out of rehab, looking for a fresh start at a new school. When he spots a former classmate, he fears his old reputation will continue to follow him.*

Oh, hi, Megan. Yeah, it is funny to see you here. How come you're at this school, too? It *is* a really small world, I guess. I can't believe you're here, too.

Uh, listen, there are some things I told people from around here this summer and . . . it would be really bad for me if . . . Well, I kind of exaggerated some stuff. I might have told people that I was on the soccer team and an honor student. I know I wasn't, but, you know . . . I wanted to get a fresh start. Make a new reputation. I'm trying to change my life for the better a little. You know things weren't very good for me before. That's why I *came* to a new school. Please, just go along with me on this. You don't have to lie, just don't say anything at all. I just want a fresh start. Will you do that for me? Please? I don't want anyone to know about what I did before. Just so you know, I'm paying everybody back for the damage, and I went to rehab. Please?

Thanks, Megan! I *really* appreciate this. I do.

CAUGHT

DENNY was caught trying to steal a TV. But that's not the worst part.

It's not funny. I can't believe I got caught. It's not funny, Mom!

Look, they dared me. I didn't even want that TV. So it's no big deal. I do some community service, and that's that.

No, I am going to keep wearing my clothes like I do. I like my pants baggy. I've told you a thousand times. Look, OK, I won't steal anymore, but you have no right to tell me I look "silly." That is a rude thing to say, Mom. This is what kids wear, Mom.

Shut up, Janelle. This is none of your business. Get lost.

Sure, I learned a lesson. I learned that if you're going to steal, make it something small, so you can hold your pants up when you run away!

It's not funny!

A LITTLE LIFT

CARL is a rule breaker who doesn't care about getting into trouble and making waves. He thrives on attention and the adventure of stealing and getting into trouble.

You worry too much about authority and getting into trouble. You have to live a little. How often do people actually get caught for breaking the law? Very rarely. And getting suspended from school is not a big deal. It's not going to keep you from getting into college. Everyone goes to college now. Even people who get suspended. Even people who get kicked out of *several* schools. But most people don't get caught. So you don't need to be scared of every little thing. Besides, you have the reputation of being really *good*, so you'd probably just get off. You can talk yourself out of a lot. *I* can talk myself out of getting in trouble a lot, and I don't have your reputation.

So take it. You want it, so take it. I'll cover you. Nothing's going to happen. And if we get caught, we'll just tell them it was an accident. I bet you'll cry, too, so we'll definitely get off. Come on, you deserve it.

POWER PLAY

FELIX is argumentative and purposefully contrary. Here, he challenges a teacher's authority.

I *do* have to have my cell phone on in class. There's a family emergency. Sure, you can call my house and ask my mom about it. She'll tell you the same thing. But if you call, you'll be blocking up the phone lines. If you must know, my grandma is in the hospital. It's critical. And if she gets sick, I need to go to the hospital to see her.

Why would my mother call the school when she can just call me directly? No, she can't just stop by on her way to the hospital. Gas costs money. Well, sure she'd have to pick me up to take me to the hospital, but that's not the point. I want to be prepared. I want to know what's going on. I've got to stay connected! This is a family emergency! See? Here's a call now. It's probably my mom saying my grandma is dead.

(Picks up the phone.) Hey. Yeah. I can catch you later. What time? Where? Are we going to the clubs? Is Amari coming? She is so hot. Yeah. OK. *(Hangs up.)*

Well, hell yeah, that was my mama. Like I said, I got to keep the line open in case of emergency!

SELF-DEFENSE 101

MARCUS has been targeted by the school bully and is searching for a way to fight back. In desperation, he's enrolled in a martial arts class.

So you're telling me that if I take these classes, I will honestly, really and truly be able to fend off any attacker? *Any* attacker. So, if you're wrong, can I get my money back? How long does it take to become a black belt? I really want to become a legal weapon—is it a legal weapon or a lethal weapon?—as soon as possible. This is really important that I do this now, and I do this fast. There's this guy who says he's going to beat me up in the parking lot on Friday. Friday! How much can you teach me by Friday? I'll come by every day. That's no problem. I just need some kind of assurance that this is going to work. This is all I have right now. You're my only hope. Do you have any death-grip holds or anything? Like a move where I can hit someone in the neck or something and freeze his entire body? Because I need something like that.

So, let's get started, OK? *(Holding his shoulder.)* Ow! That really hurt! You're supposed to be helping me here!

THE ACCUSATION

SAM isn't the most popular guy in school. Someone is spreading the rumor that he's gay since he doesn't have a girlfriend, and Sam is hurt and angry.

Why would he say that? I'm not gay! I just . . . I just don't go on dates. But it's not like I don't want to. It's just that . . . it doesn't come up. At least . . . well, I can't help it that girls aren't exactly crazy about me.

Of course I would tell you if I was homosexual! It's not— You know, this is weird. I have to admit, I think being called that is an insult. But if someone were gay, I wouldn't hate him for it! There's just no right way to say this. God, I don't know, it hurts my feelings to hear people say that! It's like they've decided it's over for me, there's no hope, I'm just going to be alone. I hate that girls don't like me! I can't help that I'm short and not, like, Brad Pitt or something!

It doesn't help that you're on their side. You think people are going to think you're gay if you hang around me, don't you? God, Tim, thanks for the support.

RUMORS

ROSE is the victim of a vicious, untrue rumor, attacking her reputation.

What are people saying about me? I don't get it! Nancy did this, didn't she? There's absolutely no truth to it! She is so mean. I can't believe she'd stoop so low. No one believes it, do they? It's totally ridiculous!

You believe me, don't you, Lynne? I know I said I like Mark, but I wouldn't do that. Two guys? One freaks me out enough. Why would I sleep with two guys at once? That's—I wouldn't do that. I'm not like that! I can't believe you actually think this is true! What a great friend you are. If I can't depend on you, who can I depend on?

Desperate. You think I'm desperate. Thanks a lot. Sure, I like Mark and I might have said I'd do *anything*, but that's just talk! You know that. I can't believe . . . This really hurts me, Lynne. I can't believe you believe this. I can't believe *anyone* believes this. This is a nightmare. Even my best friend . . . We're not friends anymore, Lynne. You've betrayed me.

NO MORE

JESSIE is a quiet girl who's had enough of her classmate bossing her around and bullying her. In the past, she's ignored the gibes and injustices, but she doesn't want to stay silent any longer.

I am so sick of you with your nose in the air, thinking you're better than me. You're not better than me. You're just a sad, old bitch. I don't know if you're insecure or something, but you should not be judging me. You should take a look at yourself. You are not perfect. You are not great. You don't have anything I don't have. Maybe you're jealous or something. You must be. Why else would you bother putting your energy into trying to pull me down? You have a problem. Go home and examine yourself. Seriously. You need to take a cold, hard look at yourself. Because I am not going to take this anymore. Get out of my face now. I don't want to talk to you anymore.

Oh, sure. I forgive you. No problem. But I won't forget.

NEW WORLD ORDER

ED imagines a less stressful world with plenty of breaks from school and work. Is this utopia possible?

Do you know in other countries kids take a year off before going to college? I feel like school is never going to end. Why do we have to go for so long? You know, my dad told me that his grandfather had to stop going to school in sixth grade, and he was upset about it! He cried when his father told him. That just sounds crazy to me. If I could get out of this, I would.

Yeah, I guess his grandfather probably had to go work after that. So that's no good. I can see why you'd be upset about that. When do we get a break? Why do you have to go right from school to work? That's no good either. We humans just don't get a break. Why do we do this to ourselves? We create the laws, right? Can't we maybe make a law where we work one year, then we take off the next year? We could all alternate years. I bet people would work harder if they knew that the next year they'd get off. Maybe it should be a rule that you only get the year off if you did a good job. Then no one would be a slob. And there would be no unemployment, too!

Man, I should be president! I'm brilliant!

STY

LOUIS's family members, including his parents, are collectors and slobs. He can't invite anyone to his house because it's so filled with junk. He's had enough.

Our house is crap. We're like one of those people that get on TV for being slobs. Why do we have to have this junk everywhere? I can't have anyone over, I can never find anything, and you get mad when I try to clean up! Other people's parents *beg* them to clean up. They would *die* if their kid voluntarily took out a vacuum. I would do that, if I could find the floor! I hate living in chaos. I don't understand how you can live like this. Why do *I* have to live like this? If you want your bedroom to be filled with junk, fine. That's your prerogative. But why should I put up with this? Most of this stuff is completely unnecessary. You probably don't know you have it. Why do we have broken vases and figurines that come with the tea bags? They're free and they're crappy. They *give* them away because no one wants them. I want to be able to walk to my room without feeling like I'm going through an obstacle course. This is not too much to ask! If you loved me, you'd do this. I can't stand living in this crazy house anymore!

MOTHER'S KEEPER

CHRIS's mother always dates men who are bad for her. Chris feels like he's the adult in his relationship with his mom.

I hate him. Sorry. But you asked me. I don't like him, Mom. He's a creep. I'm a guy, too, I can tell. He's a user. Why do you ask me what I think if you don't want to hear it? Sure, I want you to find someone. But he should be nice, Mom. You're always bringing home the wrong kind of guy for you. Find somebody nice, Mom. Nice is not boring! Nice doesn't walk out on you. Nice is reliable. Nice holds a steady job. Aren't those things important? I am not too practical! There's no such thing. Look, we need someone around here who's gonna help, not drain your wallet and make you cry. I'm sorry! But I'm telling the truth. I'm sick of this thing where you bring home some guy, I'm supposed to love him and listen to him and take his advice and see him as some kind of male role model, and then he takes your money or breaks your heart or just disappears. It's the same thing every time. You have terrible taste, Mom. Sure, you deserve love, but . . . Why do you go for these smooth-talking players? You're asking for it. You need a *nice* guy, Mom. So nice guys aren't exciting?

God, you don't make sense! You want me to be a good kid—responsible, trustworthy, hardworking—but then you tell me that these aren't good qualities in men. You say you want to keep me out of gangs, but then you go for these dangerous types. What am I supposed to think?

BLACK LIKE ME

ALEX's friend just made a racist, stereotypical statement. Alex feels like he has to set him straight and not let him get away with making assumptions based on skin color.

What do you mean, "people like *me*"? "People like me" do whatever they want. "People like me" don't conform to stereotypes. I can't believe you'd say something like that. That's so ignorant.

No, no! Don't try to justify this! Now I know who you are. You're racist. I'm just glad I know now.

Yeah, I thought I was your friend, but maybe I was your token friend. Where did you get these ideas, anyway?

Fine, fine. I'll give you another chance. But don't pull that again. I am a human being, just like you. That's all. Every person is unique; it has nothing to do with the color of their skin. I can't believe after all these years these kind of things still come up! I would maybe expect it from someone in the street, but you? I never saw this coming.

OK. I'll let it go. But you'd better get educated and get your facts straight because that kind of talk is just insulting.

THE SMELL

ROGER's roommate refuses to do laundry. Their room smells bad. Roger tries to take control of the situation and get his roommate to see the light before the problem gets toxic.

Dude, this room smells. You have to do laundry. No one likes to do laundry; but, trust me, it's *time*. You cannot wear anything on this floor ever again. Not even the underwear. *Especially* the underwear! I would not be saying this to you unless this was really important. You *have* to do laundry. Seriously. I think, even after I take a shower, I walk out of this room smelling like your socks. No girl wants to have anything to do with a guy who smells like sweaty socks. Do you want to be alone forever?

No, no, no. You cannot wait until the end of the year for your mother to do your laundry. It's *March*, man. Graduation is *months* away. I'm not kidding! I can't breathe here. I *wish* I couldn't breathe here!

What? No! I'm not going to do your laundry. Get up, get these clothes in a laundry bag, and get downstairs to the laundry room! Look, I'll give you my detergent and some quarters. I just can't take the smell anymore! If I dared to, I'd throw your dirty clothes out the window. I'm just afraid I'd get a disease in the process! Come on, you have to do this or I'll call the Environmental Protection Agency.

REBEL-IN-TRAINING

KIT is stuck between pleasing her parents and wanting to be rebellious. She's actively trying to find ways to be her own person.

I told you I wanted *red* hair. This is what I meant, Mom. Red. I don't want "Warm Auburn." Yuk! That's like a color old ladies use to cover up their gray. I want *red* hair. Other kids do it all the time! It's not *permanent.* I don't see why you have to be so uptight about it.

Well, you are being uptight! So what if my hair is a different color? Why are you acting as if this is going to damage me in some way? I'll still be the same person. And if I want my hair to go back to its natural color at some point, I just grow it out. No big deal. I can't believe I have to explain this to you! Why are so threatened by this?

I can't be your little girl forever. I have to grow up sometime. But you have this attitude like dyeing my hair is going to make me a different person, a dirty person or something. I'm still *me*, Mom. I'm just older. I'm growing up. And I have to make my own decisions.

I don't want my hair to be a "natural" color. I want *red*, Mom.

BEST STRESSED

LACEY desperately wants to be immortalized as Best Dressed in the yearbook. However, her mom is not going along with the plans.

Mom, I have to have those jeans. I have to! I am in the running for Best Dressed in the yearbook! I have to stay ahead of the trend. I have to be on the cutting edge. I *have* to have nicer clothes than anyone else! You don't understand. This is important. This is immortality. This is being acknowledged. I'm not going to be the smartest or the most popular, but this is one thing I can do! Please, Mom, I just need a little financial help from you right now. This is the difference between being a VIP and being a nobody.

I am not becoming materialistic. I don't actually care about this stuff; I just care about what it gets me. *I'd* be happy wearing jeans and a T-shirt. Well, mostly. OK. I do like all this stuff—clothes, bags, fashion—but, see, this is important to be accepted. *And*, I don't know, I've been thinking about my future, too. I think I might want to be a fashion designer. So the first step is having fabulous clothes.

Oh god, Mom, no! You're not getting this at all! If I started making my own clothes, that would be the end of me! I'd be an automatic loser!

LATER

NICK is scared of standing out and being an outcast. One of his good friends from childhood recently "came out," and Nick doesn't want to be seen with him anymore.

Look, no offense, but we can't be friends anymore. Not since . . . you know. You came out. I can't . . . I can't have people thinking I'm like you. I'm sorry, but I'm just being honest.

I know we've been friends since we were kids, and that's why it's so bad. People are thinking I'm gay, and I can't have that. I'm not. You know, guys like you are always friends with girls. You might want to check that out.

I'm trying to be helpful! Look, this isn't helping. People are looking. Don't get upset. This is just the way the world works. Yeah, of course I'm going to miss hanging out. Sure, we had some laughs. But don't you see what this is doing to me? I'm sorry about this. I am. You're the funniest guy I know. But I can't be seen with you anymore. I can't even look at you in the halls. I have to let myself have a normal life. Please, you'll find other friends. Just calm down. Well, good luck with everything. I gotta go.

CRIBS

SUNNY is the child of hippie parents visiting a very wealthy friend.

This house is amazing. Your parents must have millions. I wish I lived here! I can't even imagine living like this. No, that's a complete lie. I *always* think about living like this. I wish my parents worked harder or something. I guess that's not fair. I mean, they're OK.

You like them? That's because they're not *your* parents. I never get *anything* I want. They're like hippies. I mean, it's the twenty-first century. They didn't even grow up in the 60s. They're younger than that. I don't know why they think they need to eat organic, macrobiotic, disgusting stuff and recycle everything. Our backyard is a compost heap. Well, I'm as into the environment as the next person, really I am, but it does get ridiculous. My dad *bikes* to work. It's just embarrassing.

I *so* wish I were you. *This* is how people are supposed to live.

SICK

JULIET is quiet and shy and has one close friend that she confides in.

Marnie, do you know what cancer feels like? I was just wondering, that's all. Does it hurt, do you think? I mean, like the lump itself. Would it hurt when you touch it? How do you think I could find out?

Sure, I feel OK. I feel fine. No, I don't need to go to a doctor. I was just wondering in general.

Well . . . OK. I think I might have cancer. I have this lump, I've *had* this lump for a while, and I was hoping it would just go away. But it hasn't. I don't want to go to a doctor. I'm afraid he'll tell me it's true. Marnie, I'm so scared that it's true and I'll have to go through chemo, and I'll lose all my hair, and I'll have to live in the hospital, and, Marnie, I'm so scared that I'm going to die. I'm scared that because I've waited it's worse. I swear I can almost feel it spreading through my body whenever I think about it. What should I do? I'm so scared, Marnie!

SUBJECT INDEX

Alternative Lifestyle
Paradise, 28
Freedom of Depression, 29
Powers, 53
Who I Am, 54

Beauty/Looks
Think Less of Me, 8
And the Winner Is . . . , 11
Abominable, 13
Beast, 26
Suddenly Sexy, 42
Degrees of Normal, 56
The Trouble with Taffeta, 77
Girlie Girl, 92
The Accusation, 99
Rebel-in-Training, 107
Best Stressed, 108

Betrayal
It's My Party, Biatch, 22
The Video, 36
Blind Date, 38
Side Kick to the Gut, 33
The Mistake, 59
Betrayal, 63
Gravity, 78
Close to You, 83
Rumors, 100
Later, 109

Competition
It's My Party, Biatch, 22
Just You Wait, 24
Puzzle #87, 37
Second Best, 47
The Prize, 48
The Big Hope, 49
Best Man, 50
Quitter, 69

Dating
Girls' Night Out, 15
That Girl, 16
Come Fly with Me, 18
Possession, 21
Blind Date, 38
In the Driver's Seat, 30
Homeless, 40
Table for Three, 60
The Right Guy, 61
I Got It, 64
The Break Up, 65
Secret, 67
Don't Tell, 70
Don't Ask Me, 71
Prisoner, 91

Drugs/Alcohol
Team Player, 20
One Moment, 34
Betrayal, 63
Relax, 72
Less, 93
Beginning, 94

Eating Disorder
Full, 62

Everything and Nothing/ Randomness
Something's Missing, 10
Camp, 12
Abominable, 13
So Hot, 14
Get Reel, 84

Food/Drink
Crash, 6
Think Less of Me, 8
Full, 62
Don't Eat the Entrees, 76

Friendship

   It's My Party, Biatch, 22

   Side Kick to the Gut, 33

   Testing 1-2-3, 41

   Best Friend, 45

   Second Best, 47

   Powers, 53

   Betrayal, 63

   Emergency Repair, 66

   Unrequited, 81

   Close to You, 83

   The Accusation, 99

   Black Like Me, 105

   Later, 109

   Sick, 111

Gender Roles

   Mr. Pink Pants, 4

   Who I Am, 54

   Girlie Girl, 92

Humiliation/Mocking

   The House on the Hill, 17

   The Dress, 19

   Possession, 21

   Life on Mars, 35

   The Video, 36

   Emergency Repair, 66

   Queen Narinda, 79

   Caught, 95

   The Accusation, 99

   Rumors, 100

Illness

   Look Away, Come Closer, 9

   Testing 1-2-3, 41

   Loathing, 57

   Full, 62

   Contracting, 73

   Sick, 111

Independence/Individuality

   Camp, 12

   Hands Off, 23

   Freedom of Depression, 29

   Holding the Line, 39

   The Stand, 55

   The Trouble with Taffeta, 77

   Rebel-in-Training, 107

Internet/Technology/Science

   Plugged In, 5

   Carpel Tunnel Warrior, 7

   Life on Mars, 35

   No Techno, 43

   Close to You, 83

   Power Play, 97

Jobs

   Camp, 12

   Don't Eat the Entrees, 76

   Hairnets and a Smile, 87

Love

   Best Friend, 45

   The Mistake, 59

   Contracting, 73

   Fire at 207 North Street, 74

   Totally Adorable, 80

   Hooked, 82

   Close to You, 83

   Mother's Keeper, 104

Moving

   Moving On, 52

   Stillness, 75

Parental Demands/Conflicts

   Look Away, Come Closer, 9

   Hands Off, 23

   Paradise, 28

   Freedom of Depression, 29

   Homeless, 40

   No Techno, 43

   The Good One, 46

   The Big Hope, 49

   Plastic, 51

Moving On, 52
Who I Am, 54
The Stand, 55
Rave or Rage, 58
Table for Three, 60
Full, 62
Quitter, 69
Relax, 72
Contracting, 73
Stillness, 75
Don't Eat the Entrees, 76
The Trouble with Taffeta, 77
Gravity, 78
Combat, 86
Hairnets and a Smile, 87
The System, 89
Prisoner, 91
Sty, 103
Mother's Keeper, 104
Rebel-in-Training, 107
Best Stressed, 108
Peer Pressure
Think Less of Me, 8
Team Player, 20
One Moment, 34
Holding the Line, 39
The Prize, 48
Degrees of Normal, 56
After, 68
Don't Tell, 70
A Little Lift, 96
Self-Defense 101, 98
Later, 109
Politics/War
The Debate, 1
Open, 2
Principles, 3
Carpel Tunnel Warrior, 7
View from the Couch, 85

Combat, 86
The Past Is Past, 88
Possessions
Hands Off, 23
No Techno, 43
Plastic, 51
Emergency Repair, 66
Sty, 103
Best Stressed, 108
Cribs, 110
Racism
Don't Ask Me, 71
Black Like Me, 105
Reputation
Possession, 21
Just You Wait, 24
The Video, 36
Suddenly Sexy, 42
The Break Up, 65
Emergency Repair, 66
After, 68
Don't Tell, 70
Less, 93
Beginning, 94
The Accusation, 99
Rumors, 100
Best Stressed, 108
Roommates
Camp, 12
The Smell, 106
School/College
Principles, 3
Oversight, 44
Moving On, 52
Unrequited, 81
The Past Is Past, 88
Power Play, 97
New World Order, 102
The Smell, 106

Self-Esteem
  Think Less of Me, 8
  Look Away, Come Closer, 9
  Abominable, 13
  The End, 25
  Beast, 26
  Second Best, 47
  Degrees of Normal, 56
  Loathing, 57
  Queen Narinda, 79
Sex
  Holding the Line, 39
  The Mistake, 59
  Betrayal, 63
  After, 68
  Less, 93
  Rumors, 100
Sexism
  Mr. Pink Pants, 4
  Degrees of Normal, 56
Sexuality
  Plugged In, 5
  Who I Am, 54
  Secret, 67
  The Accusation, 99
  Later, 109
Sports
  In the Driver's Seat, 30
  The Prize, 48

The Big Hope, 49
Best Man, 50
Quitter, 69
Black Belt Betty, 90
Self-Defense 101, 98
Stealing
  Caught, 95
  A Little Lift, 96
Taking a Stand
  And the Winner Is . . . , 11
  It's My Party, Biatch, 22
  Hands Off, 23
  Life on Mars, 35
  Side Kick to the Gut, 33
  Plastic, 51
  The Stand, 55
  Stillness, 75
  Queen Narinda, 79
  Self-Defense 101, 98
  No More, 101
  Rebel-in-Training, 107
Unrequited Love
  Love with the Perfect
    Supermodel, 27
  Caller #25, 31
  Too Much, 32
  The Right Guy,61
  Unrequited, 81
  Girlie Girl, 92

THE AUTHOR

Kristen Dabrowski is an actress, writer, acting teacher, and director. She received her MFA from the Oxford School of Drama in Oxford, England. The actor's life has taken her all over the United States and England. Her other books, published by Smith and Kraus, include *The Ultimate Monologue Book for Middle School Actors Volume I: 111 One-Minute Monologues, The Ultimate Audition Book for Teens Volume III: 111 One-Minute Monologues, Twenty 10-Minute Plays for Teens Volume 1,* the *Teens Speak* series (four books), and the educational *10+* play series (six books). Currently, she lives in the world's smallest apartment in New York City. You can contact the author at monologuemadness@yahoo.com.